CW01426045

WHEN GRIEF AND LOSS WON'T SHUT UP

A GUIDE TO NAVIGATE EMOTIONAL WAVES, BUILD SELF-COMPASSION, MAKE PEACE WITH THE PAIN AND FIND JOY WITHOUT GUILT

DENA M DERENALE BETTI

CONTENTS

To my husband, Paul, my love and heart,

and to my daughters, Jenna, Julia, and Gigi, my life's greatest gifts.

To my mom, dad, and sister, whose love and wisdom

have shaped me in ways beyond measure.

You are the reason I believe in love, in possibility,

and in the power of never giving up.

Every word I write carries a piece of you.

GRIEF, LOVE, AND THE STORY
THAT CONNECTS US

It was a Sunday in March, one of those early spring days when the sun felt warmer, the air a little softer. My 14-year-old daughter Jenna had a smile that could light up a room, and that morning, the world felt normal—whole. But as the day unfolded, it became clear that life was about to fracture in ways I couldn't have imagined. The day began beautifully, but it ended as the worst day of my life.

Jenna was gone. A tragic accident took her from us, and in the instant I learned of her passing, my heart shattered into a million pieces. The physical pain of grief was almost unbearable as if my body couldn't contain the weight of my sorrow. I couldn't breathe. I couldn't think. I could only exist in that raw, excruciating moment.

In the following weeks, I tried to make sense of a world that no longer felt recognizable. People offered well-meaning words, but phrases like "you're so strong" or "I can't believe how well you're keeping it together" landed like heavy stones on an already-burdened heart. What they couldn't see was the weight I was carrying beneath the surface—the heartbreak, the exhaustion, the silent screams of grief that consumed me. Their words didn't fill the emptiness—they amplified it. I may have appeared composed on the outside, but it was a fragile facade masking the storm raging within me. The heartbreak, the confusion, and the overwhelming weight of grief felt impossible to convey. Deep down, I knew I would somehow have to figure out how to escape the darkness, even as the path forward felt unimaginable.

WHEN GRIEF BECOMES A CONSTANT COMPANION

This book is not about "getting over" loss or "moving on." Let's lay that myth to rest right now. Grief doesn't go away, it changes, evolves, and becomes a part of you. It's not something to conquer but something to live with. It becomes a constant chatter in the background of your life, sometimes whispering, sometimes roaring, but always present. It shapes the way you see the world, colors your memories, and influences even the quietest moments. Learning to live with grief isn't about silencing it—it's about learning how to listen without letting it drown you.

When Grief and Loss Won't Shut Up is a companion for the journey. It's a safe space where you can acknowledge your pain, honor your loved one, and begin to see glimmers of hope, even if they feel faint and far away. Together, we'll navigate the messy, complicated emotions of grief: the anger, the guilt, the fear, and yes, the love that remains.

Through personal stories and practical tools, I'll share what I've learned on my grief journey. I'll walk with you as you find ways to care for yourself, lean on others, and create rituals that help you remember your loved one without feeling consumed by the loss.

THE BALANCE BETWEEN LOVE AND LOSS

This book is about balance—the delicate and often elusive equilibrium between love and loss. It's about learning to carry your grief in a way that allows you to move forward without leaving behind the person who is no longer physically here.

Grief isn't linear. It's not predictable or tidy. It's a winding road with sharp turns, detours, and unexpected moments of peace. Healing doesn't mean forgetting; it means finding new ways to carry the memories, love, and connection that remain.

For me, founding the #hersmile Nonprofit in Jenna's memory became a way to express my love for her in a world where she was no longer physically here to receive it. It wasn't about finding purpose in the face of loss but finding a way to live out the boundless love I still feel for her. That love had nowhere to go, and the nonprofit became a channel—a way to honor her life, her smile, and the light she brought into the world.

Grief, for me, was never just about sadness; it was also about love—overflowing, relentless love that her absence couldn't extinguish. The nonprofit gave me a way to keep that love alive, to transform it into action, and to let it touch others in the way Jenna's love had touched me. It was a way of saying, "She's still here. Her love is still here. She is very much alive."

But I know that's my way, and we all grieve differently. For some, grief calls for stillness—a quiet honoring of their lost connection. For others, it's found in movement, creating, and doing. There's no right way to grieve, no universal formula for healing. What matters is finding your way to live with your grief, to carry it, and to honor the love that remains.

#hersmile became a guiding light for me. It reminded me that love doesn't disappear even in the darkest days—it transforms. If we choose, that love can fuel us, move us, and connect us in ways we never thought possible. And in choosing to let my love for Jenna guide me, I've found glimpses of healing—not by letting go of my grief, but by allowing that love to light the path forward.

AN INVITATION TO HEAL

Finally, this book is an invitation. It invites you to feel your emotions, embrace your unique grieving process, and let love guide you through the most challenging moments. The words aim to remind you that people see, hear, and stand with you.

Grief and love are intertwined—two sides of the same coin. And while grief can feel unbearable at times, it's also proof of the depth of your love. Together, let's explore what it means to hold space for both.

So, take a deep breath. Let's begin this journey together. It won't be easy, but you'll find strength, courage, and moments of grace you didn't think possible with every step. Because even when grief and loss feel relentless, love will always light the way forward.

1

UNDERSTANDING YOUR GRIEF JOURNEY

When you lose someone you love, it's as if the ground beneath you gives way, leaving you unsteady and uncertain in a world that feels both familiar and entirely foreign. I remember standing in my daughter's room, surrounded by the mosaic of her life—her school backpack, the clothes she wore, the small, ordinary things that once seemed so unremarkable but now carried the weight of her absence. Her perfume still lingered in the air, and for a fleeting moment, I could almost hear her laughter filling the room.

Grief has a way of bending reality. It feels like stepping into a parallel universe where your heart aches in ways you never imagined possible, and nothing feels quite the same. I realized that grief is not a single, straightforward emotion at that moment. It, too, is a mosaic, but this one is of love and longing, joy and pain, each piece impossibly tangled with the others.

This chapter explores that mosaic—a journey into the intricate dance of grief. Grief doesn't move in straight lines; it ebbs and flows, rises and falls, much like the ocean's waves. Wherever you are in your grief, I hope these pages will help you navigate their currents with compassion for yourself and the love that ties it all together.

EMBRACING THE UNPREDICTABLE WAVES

Grief is often compared to the ocean, with its tides shifting between moments of calm and healing to surges of overwhelming intensity. Similarly, C.S. Lewis captures the unpredictable nature of grief in *A Grief Observed*: "Grief is like a long valley, a winding valley where any bend may reveal a new landscape." Both analogies reflect the same truth—grief is neither predictable nor linear. Whether it feels like navigating the shifting tides of the ocean or walking through a winding valley, grief is a journey marked by unexpected changes that challenge your footing and sense of direction.

What makes grief so tricky is its unpredictability. Some days bring moments of calm and reflection, where memories of your loved one feel comforting, like a warm embrace. On other days, the weight of loss crashes over you, leaving you breathless and searching for stability. These fluctuations are not signs of failure or weakness— they're a testament to the depth of your love. A love so profound that it continues to shape your emotions and your healing. While the journey is far from linear, understanding the ebb and flow of grief can help you meet it with compassion and patience, allowing your- self to feel and heal in your own time.

And that's the thing about grief—it's as unique as the love that caused it. There's no right way to grieve, no roadmap, and no set timeline. There's no "should" regarding how you feel or move through this process. Each wave you face, whether tiny or towering, is valid. The key is to give yourself the grace to feel—whether it's sadness, anger, longing, or even moments of laughter. Grief can be chaotic, but it is also profoundly human.

While the ocean of grief may feel isolating at times, I want to tell you again that you are not alone. Many have stood where you stand, staring at the vastness of loss, unsure how to move forward. Though our journeys may not look the same as yours, our shared understanding can be a beacon—a reminder that healing is possible, even in the face of uncertainty.

So, as you navigate this sea of emotions, allow yourself to embrace the ebb and flow. There will be calm waters and crashing waves; with each one, you'll discover the strength to keep going. Within the uncertainty lies the potential for healing, growth, and finding new ways to carry the love that will always remain.

EXPECTATIONS VS. REALITY

In the immediate aftermath of Jenna's passing, I clung to the belief that time would eventually dull the sharp edges of my grief. I assured myself and my husband that this heartbreak wouldn't define us, that somehow we would not break under the heavy weight that hung over us, and that the emotional pain would eventually ebb away like a physical wound healing with time. Much like a scar, I imagined it would fade into the background, a quiet reminder of my beautiful, precious daughter. Yet, as days turned into weeks and weeks into months, I was confronted with a far different reality from my expectations. Grief was not a visitor passing through; it had settled into my bones, becoming an inherent part of my existence. I saw that my grief wasn't something to overcome but something to carry—a testament to the depth of my love for Jenna.

In the early days after Jenna's passing, I struggled to make sense of the overwhelming emotions that consumed me. The idea that grief could be "managed" or "resolved" felt impossible. It wasn't until I encountered the work of Elisabeth Kübler-Ross and David Kessler that I began to understand grief as a journey, not a destination. Their wisdom, which emphasized that grief is not a linear process, helped me reframe what I was experiencing. They reminded me that while the intensity of my sorrow might shift over time, the love I held for Jenna would always remain. Grief, I realized, wasn't something to be fixed or healed—it was a reflection of the bond that death could never break.

This understanding changed how I approached my grief. Instead of letting it immobilize me, I chose to give it movement, to channel it into something meaningful. Four months after Jenna's passing, I founded the #hersmile Nonprofit—a way to express my love for Jenna by creating something positive in a world that now felt so dark. Turning my grief into action wasn't about escaping the pain; it was about honoring Jenna's memory in a way that allowed her light to continue shining through me.

As I leaned into this journey, grief revealed an unexpected truth: it softened me in ways I never anticipated. It opened my heart to vulnerability, made me more empathetic, and deepened my relationships with those around me. Grief became a teacher, guiding me toward greater introspection and clarity about what truly mattered in my life.

Understanding your grief journey doesn't mean finding quick solutions or rushing through the pain. It means recognizing that grief is a companion, not an obstacle. Our expectations about how grief "should" look or feel often do not align with the reality of living through it. Grief evolves with you, shaping your path in ways you might not have anticipated while constantly reminding you of the love that endures beyond the loss. For me, grief became a force that transformed devastation into purpose, and it taught me that healing doesn't follow a predictable timeline. Instead, it begins with the small, meaningful steps we take toward hope, connection, and embracing the unexpected realities of this journey.

PSYCHOLOGICAL AND PHYSICAL CONNECTIONS

In the months following Jenna's passing, I was also overcome by a relentless exhaustion that went far beyond what words could adequately capture. My body felt like it was carrying an invisible weight, manifesting as aches, tightness, and profound fatigue that I couldn't shake. Every morning, I woke with a heaviness in my chest, as if my grief was compressing my very ability to breathe. Tasks that once felt simple now loomed like mountains, and my mind operated in a fog, where even the slightest thoughts felt like they were swimming upstream.

It wasn't until I began to reflect on what was happening—and came across the words of Dr. Bessel van der Kolk in *The Body Keeps the Score* —that I understood grief as more than an emotional experience. Van der Kolk's work revealed that trauma and grief take residence in the body, embedding themselves in our muscles, our breath, and our very being. This was a revelation. My body wasn't betraying me; it was grieving too. The aches, unrelenting fatigue, the tension that seemed to grip me like a vice—all of it was my body's way of expressing what my heart couldn't put into words.

Grief isn't just a feeling we experience in our minds; it's a physical entity that lives within us. We carry it in every heartbeat, every breath, and every restless night. For me, each milestone that passed without Jenna—the birthdays, the holidays, the quiet, ordinary moments—was a physical echo of her absence. My body felt her loss as deeply as my soul did, as if every cell in me were mourning the future we would never share.

Yet, within this pain, I discovered something sacred. The physicality of my grief became a testament to the depth of my love for Jenna. Each ache and moment of exhaustion reminds us of the bond we share. I began to see my body's response not as a weakness but as a profound expression of love and loss intertwined. That understanding became a turning point for me.

Grief didn't just mark the end of Jenna's physical presence in my life, it also became the way I carried her forward. Honoring Jenna's memory, celebrating her life, and ensuring her spirit remains alive transformed my grief into something living. It became my way of loving her, even amidst the shadows of loss. This was not about "moving on"; it was about moving with my grief and allowing it to deepen my connection to her, even as I navigated the pain of her absence.

THE ENORMITY OF GRIEF

Grief can feel all-encompassing and unrelenting, reshaping how you see the world and who you are within it. If you're reading this, you may know exactly what I mean. The devastation, the darkness—it feels inescapable like the enormity of it might swallow you whole. You may feel like you don't know how to move forward, or even if you want to. That's what grief does; it disorients and overwhelms you, leaving you in a place where even the simplest things feel impossible.

I understood this more deeply through my work with the #hersmile Nonprofit. Meeting families who had suffered the unimaginable brought me face-to-face with the vastness of grief and the unique ways it shows up in people's lives. I remember a father who lost his son in a tragic bicycle accident. His grief was raw, overpowering, and filled with anger—anger directed at anyone he thought might be responsible, even though it had been an accident.

In him, I saw the frenetic energy of grief, how it refuses to follow a predictable path or timeline. For some, deep sadness takes hold in grief, making it feel impossible to lift. For others, it's silence, guilt, rage, or even blame—an attempt to make sense of the unbearable.

Each person navigates their pain in their own way, but no matter how it looks for you, the heartbreak beneath it is the same.

What struck me most in those moments wasn't just the enormity of their pain but the universality of it. Grief doesn't ask you to fix it, it's not something you can fight or solve. It asks you to feel it, bear witness to its weight, and honor the love at its center. Working with grieving families taught me that my role wasn't to make their pain go away, it was to stand with them in it. To hold space for their sorrow, to let them feel seen, and to remind them that they weren't alone even in their darkest moments.

This wasn't an easy path. Sitting with others in their grief often mirrored my own heartbreak, forcing me to confront my pain in ways I wasn't always ready for. I felt like Humpty Dumpty, tumbling off the wall again and again, each fall adding another crack to an already fragile shell. Just when I thought I had pieced myself back together, another wave of sorrow would knock me down. There were days when I felt overwhelmed, questioning whether I could continue carrying both their pain and my own. But I saw this work as an extension of my love for Jenna—a way to give the love I could no longer express to her directly, even as I gathered my broken pieces and tried, once more, to hold them together.

At first, it was hard to see the connection. How could sitting in the depths of someone else's sorrow possibly be tied to my love for my daughter? But over time, I realized that giving love to another human being—offering them compassion, presence, and understanding— was my way of honoring Jenna's memory. It was my way of letting her love move through me and into the world, creating ripples of light even in the darkest places.

Grief, I realized, is a reflection of love's depth. The enormity of my loss mirrored the unbreakable bond I shared with Jenna, a connection that transcends time and space. As much as I wished it wasn't my path, it became one where I learned to hold both love and loss in the same breath. Grief wasn't an adversary to conquer—it became a companion I could walk alongside.

Creating #hersmile gave me a way to navigate this new reality, to take the pain that threatened to consume me and turn it into something meaningful. It wasn't about closure—because grief doesn't close. Instead, it became about finding movement, about ensuring Jenna's light continued to shine in a world forever changed by her absence.

If you're in the depths of grief, I want you to know that it's okay to feel lost, angry, or broken. It's okay not to know how to move forward. Grief is heavy and complex, but it's a testament to the love you hold—a love so profound that it shapes you and stays with you.

My work with #hersmile has taught me something profound: healing isn't about erasing the pain or forgetting the loss. It's about learning to carry that pain alongside the love that remains. It's about letting that love be the anchor that steadies you when everything feels impossible.

As you sit with your grief, I invite you to consider this: What if, instead of focusing on the weight of the pain, you shifted your focus to the gift of the love that created it? What if the ache in your heart could remind you of the depth of the connection you share rather than just the loss of it? This isn't about denying the pain—it's real and valid. But it's also about recognizing that the pain exists because the love is so profound.

Even in your darkest moments, when sorrow feels like it has taken over everything, love is still there. It's intertwined with your grief, woven into every tear and every memory. And if you let it, that love can guide you. It can help you take the next step, no matter how small, and remind you that you don't have to do this by yourself.

Take a moment to reflect on that love—let it reveal the gift within it and guide the way you carry both grief and hope into the world.

As you reflect, I invite you to ask yourself these questions:

1. **What did this person bring into my life that I might not have experienced without them?**
2. **What are some of the most meaningful memories we created together, and how do they still bring light into my life?**
3. **What qualities or values did they embody that continue to inspire me or shape who I am today?**
4. **How can I honor the love we shared in how I live my life now?**
5. **What small moments or lessons from our time together remind me of the beauty of our connection?**

These questions open the door to possibility, shining a light on the gifts your loved one brought into your life. They can help you see how love continues, how connection endures, and how even in grief, there is space for meaning, healing, and a future shaped by their presence.

SUDDEN BURSTS AND EMOTIONAL FLUCTUATIONS

Grief can sneak up on you in the most unexpected moments, often when you think you've found a steady rhythm in its aftermath. It doesn't arrive with fanfare—it's more like a quiet, persistent knock on the door of your heart, asking to come in. I remember walking through the grocery store, lost in the mundane task of checking items off my list, when I turned a corner into the cereal aisle and saw Jenna's favorite cereal. In that instant, a flood of memories washed over me—waking her up for school in the mornings, singing "Rise and Shine" as she groaned and buried her head under the covers. I could see her sitting at the kitchen table, still half-asleep, pouring that cereal into her bowl while I packed her lunch. Those quiet, everyday moments that seemed so ordinary at the time now felt like treasures etched into my heart. That cereal box wasn't just a box, it was a doorway back to her presence, to a time when her laughter and energy filled the air. It was a memory, a connection, a reminder of how her spirit shaped the fabric of my life.

Small and seemingly ordinary moments remind you how deeply your life is intertwined with the memories of the person who is no longer physically here. They don't just live in the significant milestones; they're tucked into the everyday moments—breakfasts, errands, inside jokes, and family traditions. And when grief catches you off guard like this, it can feel disorienting and lonely. The world around you seems to have moved on, yet there you are, standing in the middle of the grocery store, trying to hold back tears over a cereal box.

The emotional rollercoaster of grief is as exhausting as it is unpredictable. One moment, a tidal wave of sadness overcomes you; the next, you find yourself laughing unexpectedly at a memory or feeling a fleeting moment of joy. These fluctuations can be confusing and leave you wondering if you're "doing grief right." I'll never forget my first Thanksgiving without Jenna. The absence was tangible, like a hollow space at the table that no amount of food or conversation could fill. After our meal, I had to retreat upstairs to collect myself, and as I did, I overheard someone ask, *"What's wrong with her?"* That question cut through me, not because they meant harm, but because it underscored how isolating grief can feel when others don't understand its depth or its persistence.

And this is what I know: grief doesn't follow a timeline or adhere to a schedule. It shows up when it wants to, often catching you off guard, demanding to be felt. And while it's hard—so incredibly hard—these moments, as painful as they are, remind you that grief and love are two sides of the same coin. The ache you feel is a reflection of the depths of your connection, and while grief can't be rushed, it deserves the space to move through you however and whenever it needs to. Sometimes, it finds you in the most unexpected places—like a cereal aisle—where a simple box can unlock a flood of memories, or at a holiday meal, where an empty seat speaks louder than words. These moments remind you of the love that will forever connect you to your loved one.

JEFF'S STORY: LIVING IN THE SHADOWS OF LOVE AND LOSS

Jeff sat in his recliner, staring at the Christmas tree glowing softly in the dimly lit room. The ornaments twinkled as if whispering memories from every Christmas past. Karen had decorated it just as she always had—perfectly balanced, warm, and full of life. She had arranged the nativity on the mantel, tied velvet ribbons around the staircase, and even placed their usual bowl of peppermint bark on the coffee table. Everything was just as it should be.

But one week later, everything changed.

The doctor's voice still echoed in Jeff's mind, delivering the words he wasn't ready to hear. The cancer had spread. It was aggressive. There was nothing more they could do. He had sat in the sterile white office, gripping Karen's hand, but she had only squeezed his back, her touch stronger than he expected for a woman receiving such devastating news.

Later that night, Jeff had stood right where he was now, in front of the same tree, watching the lights flicker as if they, too, were holding back tears. "I don't know how to do this," he had whispered into the silence, the weight of it all pressing down on his chest.

But Karen had known. Even in her last days, when she should have been resting, she had spent her fleeting energy worrying about him. About their family.

He hadn't known what she had done until Christmas morning when their children and grandchildren gathered as they always did. Jeff had gone to reach for a present when he noticed a small white box with his name written in Karen's handwriting. His hands trembled as he opened it, revealing a folded letter inside.

"My Jeff,
I know you're going to struggle with this first Christmas without me, but I need you to promise me something. Don't let grief steal what we built together. I will always be in this home, in our family, in the laughter of our grandkids. I will be there in the lights, in the giving, in the love that never fades. Christmas was always ours, and it always will be. So please, my love, keep the tree lit for me. Always.
Yours forever, Karen."

Tears blurred his vision as he looked around the tree, suddenly seeing more boxes—one for each of their children, one for each grandchild. Even in her last days, she had made sure to leave pieces of herself wrapped beneath the tree, little shadows of her love tucked into ribbons and paper.

Now, a year later, Jeff stood in front of the same Christmas tree, his fingers brushing against the silver bell ornament Karen had bought the year they were married. She was still there. Not in the way he longed for, but in the traditions she had built, in the lights she once strung, in the way Christmas would forever hold her touch.

He turned to the fireplace, where Karen's stocking still hung beside his. He had thought about packing it away, but something held him back. Maybe it was the promise he had made to her. Maybe it was the simple truth that her love would always be part of this season, woven into the meaning of Christmas itself.

Jeff reached for the small box he had set under the tree earlier that evening. It wasn't much, just a letter, but this time, it was for her.

He knelt beside the tree, placed the box near her stocking, and whispered, *"The tree is still lit, Karen. I love you always."*

REFLECTION AND ACTION

As you navigate this shadow of absence, here are some questions to help you connect with the love that still exists amidst the loss:

1. **What are some of the small, everyday moments you shared that comfort you when you think of them?**
2. **How can you honor their presence during milestones that feel especially difficult?**
3. **How can you incorporate their memory into your daily life through rituals, storytelling, or keepsakes?**
4. **What is one thing you can do today to focus on the light they brought into your world rather than just the shadow of their absence?**
5. **How can you offer yourself compassion when grief feels overwhelming in unexpected moments?**

These reflections are about leaning into the love that continues living in their absence. While the shadow of absence can feel heavy, it is also a profound reminder of how deeply they mattered—and how deeply they still do. Take these moments as opportunities to honor your shared connection and allow their love to guide you forward and to fill you, even amid the ache.

FINDING THE RIGHT BALANCE

One of the families I met shared a story that profoundly illuminated what it means to find balance after loss. A mother grieving the loss of her young son turned to painting as a way to process her pain. For her, each canvas was more than just an outlet for sorrow—it was a tribute to his life and a celebration of the love they will always share.
  Art allowed her to hold both the deep ache of grief and the enduring love she had for her son. It allowed her grief to move through her, to be heard, acknowledged and cared for—offering a space where sorrow and love could be displayed on a canvas.

I also met a father who transformed his heartbreak into action after losing his daughter. He began organizing charity runs in her memory. For him, the balance also came in movement—each step a tribute to her joy and a way to channel his grief into purpose. Running didn't erase his pain, but it gave him a sense of direction, a way to carry his love for her in the world. Both of these stories remind me that balance doesn't mean "fixing" your grief or stuffing it away. It's about finding ways to integrate it into your life, to hold space for both the pain and the love in a meaningful and sustainable way. That balance comes from honoring the journey of your life—not allowing it to break you, but to break you open, deepening your compassion and empathy for our shared human experience.

These examples taught me that balance is not a destination, it's practice. It's about finding rituals, actions, or moments that allow you to honor the weight of your loss while staying connected to the light of your love. Balance doesn't look the same for everyone, and it doesn't have to. What matters is finding something that helps you steady yourself, even if just for a moment, as you move through the unpredictable terrain of grief.

For me, balance has been about learning how to honor Jenna's memory out into the world while also living a life reflecting the love and joy she brought me. A life she would be proud of. Some days, the weight of her absence feels unbearable, but on others, her love feels so present that it lifts me, guiding me forward. I've come to see that balance isn't about erasing the pain or forgetting—it's about weaving her memory into the fabric of our lives in a way that allows both love and grief to coexist within the framework of our family.

If you are walking this path, please reflect on what balance might look like for you. It could be a creative outlet that allows you to express your emotions or an act of service that keeps your loved one's spirit alive. Perhaps it's simply permitting yourself to grieve on your terms without judgment or expectation.

Finding balance with your emotions after a loss requires both reflection and self-compassion. It's about understanding how grief and love can coexist in an authentic and healing way. To help you explore what balance looks like for you, consider asking yourself:

- **What emotions am I avoiding, and how might facing them gently help me feel whole?**
- **What activities or rituals help me feel connected to my loved one who has passed, and how can I incorporate them into my daily life?**
- **When I experience moments of joy or peace, do I embrace them entirely, or do I feel guilt? How might I release that guilt and honor the love that still exists?**
- **What boundaries do I need to set—with myself or others—to create space for my grief and healing?**
- **How can I practice self-compassion on the days when the weight of grief feels overwhelming?**

Healing begins when you permit yourself to carry grief and love together, to let them coexist as reminders of our humanity. This is where balance lives—not in choosing one emotion over the other, but in allowing both to have space within you. It's not about forgetting or moving on—it's about embracing the fullness of your emotions and recognizing that grief and love are intertwined threads of the same story. Trust that even in your darkest moments, the light of love will continue to guide you forward, offering glimpses of hope and connection amid the pain. You find balance in this delicate dance, where sorrow and love meet to shape your path toward healing.

THE UNCHARTED LANDSCAPE OF GRIEF

"I never thought this would happen to us—never imagined that grief would find its way into our family, into our lives."

— BILL CLEGG, DID YOU EVER HAVE A FAMILY

You don't choose grief—it finds you, thrusting you into an uncharted world with no map, no compass, no survival guide to tell you what comes next. There's no class to prepare you for the weight of loss, no GPS to navigate the unpredictable terrain. Each path is different, shaped by the love you shared, the circumstances of your loss, and the irreplaceable nuances of your relationship. What worked for someone else may not work for you because grief is as individual as the bond that you share. It often arrives without warning, defying logic and timelines, often overwhelming you when you feel most unprepared. And yet, within this vast and unfamiliar landscape, there is something sacred—an invitation to sit with the fullness of your emotions, to honor your love in new ways, and to find meaning in a connection that death cannot sever.

That's the thing about grief—it doesn't follow a single path, and neither will you. The ways you move forward will be as unique as the love you carry. There is no "right" way to grieve—only the way that helps your heart to speak its truth. Grief, for all its enormity and winding roads, is inseparable from love. Every ache, wave of longing, and moment of emptiness reflects the depth of the connection you shared and, how I see it, will always share. A connection so profound that it demands acknowledgment, even as it challenges you to endure the weight of its absence.

As you walk this path, remember that you are not alone. There is a vast, unseen community of others who understand the depths of your pain, who share in the longing, the questioning, and the search for meaning. In these shared experiences, there is strength. Together, we can navigate the unpredictable, finding courage not in escaping grief but facing it—with tenderness, honesty, and the quiet knowing that love endures, even in the face of immeasurable loss.

2

NAVIGATING EARLY GRIEF

The call came in, shattering what little sense of reality I had left. It was from Donor Network West, the California Organ Donor Organization. My mind couldn't process how I had been brought to *'this call'*. How was this happening? How was I in this conversation? I wasn't ready to speak, let alone make decisions about Jenna's body. But there was no time to prepare.

The last thing any parent wants to have is this conversation. But in the midst of my devastation, I knew—Jenna would have wanted me to have it. She would have wanted her life to serve someone else's.

I wasn't prepared—how could anyone be?—for the questions they asked. They went through every possible organ, every tissue, every gift that could be passed on to another person. Her heart, her lungs, her corneas, her skin. Each question was a fresh cut, each answer a brutal reminder that she was truly gone. I wanted to scream, to hang up, to refuse to face this reality. But then I thought of the people on the other side of this call—those waiting, hoping, praying for a chance at life. I imagined a mother, sitting beside her child's hospital bed, clinging to hope. A man desperate for a new heart so he could watch his grandchildren grow up. I couldn't spare myself this pain, but maybe I could spare another family from enduring it.

So, I answered their questions. Through sobs. Through shaking hands. Through a grief so deep I wasn't sure I'd survive it. And in that unbearable moment, I found the tiniest sliver of peace. Jenna's life would not end entirely. Somewhere, pieces of her would live on —giving breath, giving sight, giving hope to someone else.

A few days later, we learned that Jenna's organs and tissues could not be gifted. Her body had gone too long without oxygen. After everything, after mustering the strength to make those impossible decisions—it wasn't meant to be. Another crushing wave of grief hit me, stealing whatever air I had left. I had wanted, so desperately, for some part of her to keep living, for another family to be spared the pain we were drowning in. That hope was gone.

And yet, again, something shifted in me that day. Even though Jenna's physical gifts could not be passed on, the possibility of sharing her light, her love—her as a gift to the world—took flight within me. I realized that Jenna's impact wasn't measured in what she left behind physically, but in how she lived, how she loved, and how I could carry that love forward. That part of her would never be lost.

Her presence, her spirit, her boundless love—they were not tied to her body I realized. They lived with the people who loved her. And they would live in me, as long as I kept finding ways to share her light with the world.

EARLY GRIEF: WHEN FEELING IS THE LAST THING YOU WANT TO DO

Grief isn't a puzzle to be solved or a wound that simply heals—it's a journey that unfolds in its own way, in its own time. And in the earliest days of grief, it can feel like an impossible journey, one you never asked to take. In those first moments, hours, and days, shock takes over. Your mind struggles to comprehend what your heart already knows. You may feel completely numb, as if your body is moving through the motions while your spirit remains frozen in disbelief. Or perhaps it's the opposite—the pain is so immediate, so unbearable, that you can barely breathe.

For Cam and Bill, the world had been certain just days before. Their daughter, Sophie, had been diagnosed with Aplastic Anemia, a blood disorder. It had been a terrifying diagnosis at first, but the doctors reassured them: It was treatable. The outlook was good, and Sophie was expected to live a full, beautiful life. They clung to that hope, convinced that science and medicine would protect their daughter's future.

Then, in a cruel twist, everything changed. A sudden infection, something minor for most children, took hold of her fragile immune system, spiraling out of control before anyone could stop it. Within days, the fight was over.

They had no time to prepare. No time to imagine a world where Sophie wasn't in it. One moment, she was their vibrant little girl, twirling in the living room with her fairy wings and giggling at her own reflection. The next, she was gone. Just like that.

And amid their unimaginable grief, life continued. There were still three other children who needed them. Basketball games still needed to be attended, dance shoes still needed to be tied, and lunches still needed to be packed. Cam and Bill moved through the motions, feeling like strangers in their own lives. How could everything outside their home go on as if nothing had changed, when inside, everything had shattered?

When Jenna passed, I felt the same way. In the morning, she was here. By the afternoon, she was gone. There was no warning, no slow progression into loss—just a before and an after. And in that after, I had a choice. I could shut down, disconnect, and let the pain swallow me whole. Or I could make a quiet, fragile promise to myself: I will not let this destroy me.

That didn't mean I had to be strong. It didn't mean I had to have all the answers. It simply meant I would allow myself to take the next breath, the next step, without turning away from what had happened.

Feeling is often the last thing you want to do. The weight of grief is so enormous that allowing yourself to truly feel the depths of it might seem like it will crush you entirely. Survival instincts take over, pushing the pain aside just to make it through the day. And that's okay. There is no right or wrong way to grieve in those early days. But as time passes, the way we navigate grief shapes our healing. Turning toward soul-nurturing practices, whether through connection, reflection, or self-compassion, can help us find light in the darkness without causing ourselves more pain.

In those earliest days, it wasn't about fully feeling—that would come later. It was about staying open. Open to the smallest glimmers of light. Open to receiving support. Open to letting love, in whatever form it arrived, hold me and my family up when I could no longer hold us all up myself. And that love came in waves—from family, from friends, from a community that wrapped itself around us in ways we could never have anticipated.

If you are in the early days of grief, know that you do not have to have it all figured out right now. You do not have to make sense of it, find meaning in it, or even believe that you will survive it. But if you can, try to stay open. Not to hope, not to healing—not yet—but simply to the love that still exists around you. That love doesn't vanish with loss; instead, it shifts, waiting for you to lean on it when you're ready.

Grief will always be a part of your story, but in time, it does not have to be the weight that holds you down. Instead, it can be the force that gently, patiently, carries you forward.

I remember one morning, months after Jenna passed when I realized I had laughed—just for a moment. It wasn't forced, and it wasn't hollow. It was small, fleeting, but real. And then came the guilt. How could I laugh in a world where she was gone? I couldn't reconcile the weight of my grief with the sudden lightness of that moment. It felt like a betrayal, as if joy and sorrow weren't allowed to exist together. But over time, I learned they do. Grief doesn't erase love, and joy doesn't erase loss. Healing isn't about choosing one over the other. It's about learning to hold them both and still finding a way forward.

There's no map for this journey, no set path that guarantees healing. But there is hope. At first, it may feel distant, barely flickering—but it is there. It might find you in the warmth of the sun on your skin when you step outside for the first time in days, in the smell of morning coffee brewing, reminding you of a life that once felt normal, or at the moment when a friend texts, "I'm thinking of you," and for a second, you feel less alone.

Hope also lives in the small acts of kindness you allow yourself to accept. A meal dropped off at your doorstep when you don't have the energy to cook. The quiet presence of a friend who sits beside you without needing to fill the silence. The knowing nod from someone who has walked this path before you. These things may seem small, but in the vast emptiness that grief can bring, they are lifelines.

I used to sit in Jenna's room, afraid to touch anything, as if moving something out of place would erase the last traces of her. But one day, I picked up her velour sweatshirt, the one she had worn so often, it still held the shape of her shoulders. As I brought it to my face, her perfume lingered in the fabric—a scent so familiar it nearly broke me. I closed my eyes, breathing it in, half expecting to turn around and see her standing there. And in that moment, I realized something: she wasn't just in the past, she was with me, always.

In time, you'll see that hope also lives in the connections you nurture —not just with others, but with yourself. Be patient with the process. You don't need to rush to find meaning or purpose. It will come in its own time, in its own way. And as you take this journey, you may discover that your pain, though heavy, can be transformed. It can live in that possibility, and it can be woven into the fabric of your life in a way that honors the bond you share and the love that will always remain.

For now, just take the next step, no matter how small. Let the love you carry guide you forward, one breath, one moment, one day at a time.

NEGATIVE STRATEGIES TO 'NOT FEEL' AND NON-SOUL-HEALING COPING SKILLS

When grief feels unbearable, it's natural to seek ways to numb the pain. But some coping mechanisms, while providing temporary relief, can ultimately prolong suffering and hinder the healing process.

I remember when my sister and a handful of friends attended a grief support group. One woman in the group shared her story—how she had turned to anti-depressant medication to help her through the darkness. For 18 months, the medication dulled the sharp edges of her pain, allowing her to function. But after a while, she realized she felt numb, as if she were frozen in place. When she made the decision to stop taking the medication, something unexpected happened —she truly *felt* her pain for the first time. It was raw, overwhelming, and unfiltered. And yet, she knew at that moment that she had done herself a disservice by delaying the process of grieving. She hadn't avoided the pain; she had only postponed it.

Her story stayed with me as a reminder that while numbing strategies may offer temporary relief, they don't allow for true healing. Only by allowing ourselves to feel, process, and move through the pain—rather than around it—can we begin to heal. Yet, like her, many people turn to coping mechanisms that seem helpful in the moment but ultimately keep grief bottled up. Here are some common negative coping strategies to be mindful of:

1. Avoidance and Emotional Suppression

- Keeping excessively busy to avoid thinking or feeling.
- Burying emotions instead of expressing them.
- Pretending to be "fine" to avoid difficult conversations.

2. Substance Use and Self-Medication

- Relying on alcohol, drugs, or excessive medication to numb emotions.
- Overuse of sleep aids or stimulants to escape reality.
- Emotional eating or severe appetite suppression.

3. Isolation and Withdrawal

- Cutting off from family and friends who offer support.
- Avoiding places, conversations, or memories that trigger emotions.
- Refusing help, even when feeling overwhelmed.

4. Risky or Self-Destructive Behaviors

- Engaging in reckless driving or dangerous activities.
- Self-harm or putting oneself in harm's way.
- Ignoring health, skipping medical care, or neglecting self-care.

5. Overattachment to the Past

- Keeping a rigid hold on grief without allowing for movement.
- Feeling guilty for moments of happiness or healing.
- Refusing to acknowledge a future without a loved one.

6. Seeking Numbness Through Screens and Distractions

- Binge-watching TV or scrolling endlessly on social media to avoid emotions.
- Overworking to avoid downtime and reflection.
- Obsessively gaming or engaging in excessive online behaviors.

7. Anger and Blame

- Constantly directing anger at others or the world.
- Blaming oneself or others excessively for what happened.
- Holding onto resentment instead of processing emotions.

8. Denial and Refusal to Acknowledge Loss

- Refusing to acknowledge the reality of the loss.
- Acting as if nothing has changed and forcing "normalcy."
- Dismissing grief as a weakness instead of recognizing it as love transformed.

While negative coping strategies may temporarily dull the pain, they ultimately keep grief trapped rather than allowing it to evolve. True healing requires facing grief in a way that honors both the love and the loss. During this time, gentle soul-healing practices can offer quiet support, even when deeper healing feels impossible. Finding ways to create space for healing, however small, can make a difference as you navigate grief, and we will explore this more deeply in a later chapter. The most important thing to remember is that grief is not about finding a way around the pain but learning to carry it with grace, knowing that love remains.

ACKNOWLEDGING THE INITIAL SHOCK AND NUMBNESS

In the immediate aftermath of losing a loved one, it's common to experience shock and numbness. This response serves as a protective mechanism—a way for the brain to buffer the impact of over-whelming pain. When we experience profound emotional trauma, our nervous system goes into survival mode, prioritizing basic func-tions while slowing down emotional processing. This is the body's way of preventing a complete emotional collapse, allowing us to absorb the reality of the loss at a pace we can handle.

I remember my legs going weak beneath me, my vision blurring as nausea surged through my gut. The moment Paul's panicked voice rang through the phone, something inside me shifted. My body knew before my mind could comprehend. This was bad. This was unimaginable. This was something I wasn't ready to face.

Somehow, I moved. I ran, stumbling over my labrador Pepper, my breath ragged, my hands shaking so violently I could barely hold my phone. The world around me was distorted—sounds muffled, instructions on where to go blurred, time both speeding up and slowing down. By the time I reached the scene of the accident, a crowd had gathered, their faces twisted in horror.

Paramedics moved with quiet urgency, their voices a blur against the pounding in my ears. My breath caught in my throat as my gaze followed their movements—then landed on what they surrounded.

I stopped. My feet refused to move forward. A primal scream built inside me, but no sound came out. My mind refused to process what my eyes were seeing. This couldn't be real. This couldn't be Jenna.

I don't remember how I got closer, but suddenly, I was there. The world tilted, my knees buckled, and my new reality whirled inside me. Then a deafening silence filled my head. Everything in me rejected the truth, yet the truth was right in front of me.

Shock wrapped itself around me like a thick fog, dulling the sharp edges of reality. My body felt disconnected from my mind, as if I were floating outside myself, watching someone else fall apart. This wasn't me. This wasn't my life. This wasn't my daughter.

But it was.

The numbness that followed wasn't just emotional, it was physical. My limbs felt heavy, my hands trembled uncontrollably, a chill fell over my body, and I began to shake uncontrollably. I couldn't eat. I couldn't sleep. I couldn't think beyond the next breath, the next step, the next impossible moment without Jenna.

And yet, even in those first days, when the weight of grief felt unbearable, I came to understand something: this shock, this numbness, wasn't a failure to keep things together. It was my mind's last defense against the unbearable truth. A survival mechanism, allowing me to absorb my loss in pieces rather than all at once.

I was protecting myself the only way my body knew how. And in time, as the numbness faded, the rawness of grief would take its place. But in those early days, the numbness was mercy.

COMMON PHYSICAL SYMPTOMS OF EARLY GRIEF

Grief doesn't just live in your heart and mind—it takes root in your body. In the earliest days, it can manifest in ways that catch you off guard, as if your body is grieving right alongside you. Your legs may feel weak, your chest tight, your stomach unsettled. You might shake without realizing it, feel cold, struggle to catch your breath, or feel crushing exhaustion despite having barely moved. Grief isn't just an emotional experience, it's a full-body response to loss. It disrupts sleep, appetite, and even basic functions as if your body itself is resisting the reality of what has happened.

We often don't realize how deeply intertwined our emotions and physical state are, yet language has long reflected the way grief physically affects us:

- **A broken heart** – The ache in your chest that makes breathing feel heavy.
- **Gut-wrenching loss** – The nausea or tightness in your stomach that comes with deep sorrow.
- **Weak in the knees** – The feeling of instability, as if your body can't hold you up.
- **A lump in your throat** – The sensation of being unable to swallow past the pain.
- **Crushed by grief** – The weight on your chest that makes it hard to take a full breath.
- **Shaken to the core** – The trembling, chills, or physical unrest that accompanies emotional shock.
- **Drained or Running on empty** – The profound exhaustion that makes even small tasks impossible.
- **Heavy-hearted** – The deep, lingering sadness that feels like a weight inside you.

These expressions exist because grief is not just something we feel— it's something our bodies endure. For many, the shock of loss triggers the fight, flight, or freeze response—your nervous system flooding with adrenaline, even though there's no action to take, no enemy to fight, no escape to make. Others feel completely drained, their limbs heavy as if weighed down by the grief itself. Some experience dizziness, headaches, or an eerie sense of numbness, where everything feels distant and unreal. This isn't weakness—it's the body's way of coping.

Recognizing these physical reactions can help you navigate them with greater awareness and self-compassion, reassuring you that you are not 'losing it' but instead moving through the natural stages of grief. While everyone's experience is unique, here are some common physical symptoms of grief that may surface in the days, weeks, and even months after loss:

- **Dizziness or lightheadedness** – A sudden rush of adrenaline or hyperventilation can make you feel unsteady.
- **Nausea or loss of appetite** – The body's response to stress often affects digestion, making food unappealing.
- **Chest tightness or shortness of breath** – Anxiety and grief can cause physical pain, mimicking heart attack symptoms.
- **Exhaustion or insomnia** – Your nervous system is overwhelmed, making sleep difficult or causing deep fatigue.
- **Trembling or weakness** – A surge of adrenaline or emotional shock may cause the body to shake or feel unstable.
- **Body aches and headaches** – Grief tension can manifest in sore muscles, headaches, or flu-like symptoms.
- **Forgetfulness or difficulty concentrating** – Your brain is in survival mode, making simple tasks feel impossible.

These symptoms can be normal responses to grief, fluctuating unpredictably. However, if they persist for an extended period, they may indicate complications with grief—something we will explore in a later chapter.

PRACTICAL TIPS FOR COPING WITH EARLY GRIEF

- **Establish Simple Routines** – Even small tasks like making tea in the morning, showering, getting out of your pajamas, and taking a short walk can create a sense of stability.
- **Accept Help Without Guilt** – Allow friends and family to assist with meals, childcare, or daily responsibilities. You do not have to carry this alone.
- **Prioritize Basic Needs** – Even if food has lost its appeal, try to eat something small or drink a nutritious smoothie. Sip water throughout the day. Rest when you can.
- **Acknowledge the Physical Impact** – Recognizing that grief is taking a toll on your body can help you be more patient and compassionate with yourself.

Early grief is disorienting, and in those first days, survival is enough. If all you can do is wake up and move through the next minute, that is enough. You are carrying something heavy, but you are not carrying it alone.

THE BRIDGE BETWEEN ISOLATION AND HEALING

Shock and numbness can be so consuming that, for many, retreating into isolation feels like the only way to survive. In those early days, the world can feel too loud, too fast, and too indifferent to the magnitude of your loss and how you are feeling. Conversations feel unbearable—how can people go on with their lives while yours feels like it has shattered? Even well-meaning words can feel like daggers, unintentionally minimizing the weight of what you carry.

I remember how people would refer to Jenna's passing as *the thing that happened.* As if it were an event, something that could be named and put away like a book on a shelf. But there was no neat label for this kind of *thing.* There was no singular event, it was a daily, living experience. A constant ache. A before and an after that I never asked for. And so, like so many who grieve, I had to fight myself from withdrawing.

WHY ISOLATION FEELS LIKE A SAFE HAVEN

For many, isolation has a provocative, almost gravitational pull, luring you into its quiet refuge where no one can misunderstand your pain, mistreat your feelings, or minimize your loss. It feels safe, like a cocoon where you can exist without expectation, without the weight of forced trivial conversations or well-meaning but hollow reassurances. When everything else has been ripped away, isolation can seem like the only thing you can control—a space where the world stops asking you to move forward when you barely know how to exist.

- **Words Feel Too Sharp** – People's attempts to offer comfort may fall painfully short. Words like *"She's in a better place"* or *"He lived a long life"* can feel like a dismissal rather than a balm. The safest place becomes solitude, where no one can say the wrong thing and where landmines are avoided.
- **The Energy to Engage Feels Impossible** – Conversations require effort, and in the wake of your loss, even the smallest interactions can be exhausting and feel like they lack meaning. The idea of making small talk or answering, *"How are you?"* when the answer is *"How do you think I am?"* can be unbearable.
- **The World Feels Disconnected from Your Pain** – Watching people continue with their daily lives—going to work, laughing at a joke, making plans—can feel surreal when your own world has stopped turning. Isolation becomes a way to create distance from the stark contrast between their reality and yours.

I used to be able to nod along to small talk, feign mild interest in the latest reality TV drama or partake in the hype of an upcoming football game. But after Jenna's passing, those conversations became so meaningless to me. Someone would ask if I had seen *Survivor* last night, and I'd stare at them blankly, wondering how on earth we were discussing such things when my world had crumbled into dust. I wanted to shake people and scream, "Don't you see? None of this matters!"

Of course, it wasn't their fault. Life kept moving on for them, even as mine had screeched to a halt. But I felt stranded—like I had been thrust into some parallel universe where connection no longer lived in the shallow waters of superficial conversation. It lived in the raw, unfiltered depths of grief and love and the meaning behind life itself.

I resented those lighthearted exchanges at first, convinced I would never care about anything hollow and insignificant again. But as time passed, I realized it wasn't small talk itself that I despised—it was the disconnection I felt from a world that no longer made sense to me. I craved depth, authenticity, the kind of conversations where people spoke from their souls instead of diving into the latest pop culture.

Grief had shifted everything inside me. It had broken me apart and reassembled me into someone new—someone who no longer had the energy for the surface-level but longed for something real. And in that longing, I found my way back—not to the world as it was, but to the version of it where meaning, connection, and love were all that truly mattered.

WHEN ISOLATION STOPS SERVING YOU

In the beginning, withdrawing may feel necessary and in the beginning when grief feels unbearable, the instinct to retreat is understandable. Isolation can feel like control, a way to shield yourself from a world that doesn't understand your pain or no longer *gets you*. But while it may feel protective, in the end, isolation can also deepen suffering, allowing sorrow to settle in without movement, without release—like a river that has stopped flowing, turning stagnant and heavy with time.

- **Connection is a lifeline.** It doesn't erase grief, but it allows it to breathe. When we share our pain—whether in a whisper, a journal, or a conversation—it shifts, even if only slightly. It's no longer trapped inside, pressing down with nowhere to go.
- **Grief needs witnesses.** Not to fix it, not to make it disappear, but to acknowledge its presence, to help you carry a weight that is nearly impossible to bear alone. When someone listens without trying to fix or minimize your grief, when they simply sit beside you in the heaviness of loss, they become a mirror for the power of love and care, reflecting back the importance of allowing love to find its way into your world again. In their presence, you are reminded that connection is still possible, that opening your heart—however cautiously—creates space for support, for kindness, and for the quiet reassurance that you don't have to carry grief alone.
- **And while not everyone will understand, someone will.** There are people who have walked this road before you. A support group, a friend who has also lost, a therapist who knows how to hold space—these connections remind you that your grief is uniquely yours, but you do not have to navigate it alone. Connection brings movement and movement—even the smallest step—prevents grief from becoming a life sentence of suffering. It offers the possibility of finding moments of light, of feeling less alone in the vastness of loss.

Reaching out, even in the smallest way, is an act of courage. It's a quiet acknowledgment that love doesn't end with loss—that life, though forever changed, still holds space for connection. Like a butterfly emerging from its cocoon, transformed by its journey, grief reshapes you. It may feel fragile, unfamiliar, even uncertain at first, but in that transformation, new ways to take flight begin to unfold. You are not who you were before, but you are still capable of moving forward—carrying love with you, allowing it to lift you, and, in time, discovering that even in loss, there is space to soar.

A NEW WAY FORWARD

So how do you move beyond isolation when the world still feels like it is too much? Slowly. Gently. In the smallest of ways.

In the early days of grief, even the idea of connection may feel like too much work—like stepping into sunlight after being in the dark for too long. It's blinding and hard to see. But to your surprise, the world keeps spinning, conversations continue, and somehow people expect you to engage, but you're not the same person you were before. And yet, while solitude can feel like a sanctuary, staying there too long can make grief feel even heavier and lonelier than it was before.

And here's the ironic part—the part no one really talks about: re-entering the world after loss feels unfair. It shouldn't be on you to make others feel comfortable around your grief, but too often, that's exactly what happens. I remember the first time I walked into the grocery store after Jenna passed and spotted someone I casually knew. I saw the hesitation in their body language and the way their eyes darted away before reluctantly meeting mine. I could feel the weight of their discomfort, their uncertainty about what to say. And I hated it. I hated that I had to be the one to break the silence, to smile first, to ease *their* unease when my own world had just been shattered. It felt like another cruel layer of loss—not only had my daughter been taken from me, but now, I had to navigate this strange, fractured version of reality where my grief made other people uncomfortable around me.

So yes, connection feels like work. And it's work you never asked for. But the alternative—staying in the isolation that grief so easily lures you into—can be even heavier and more heartbreaking. The key is to move forward in a way that honors both your pain and your capacity in this moment, no matter how small that step might be.

Find Your Safe People

Not everyone will know what to say, and some will say all the wrong things. But there will be a few who don't try to fix you, who don't rush you toward healing, who simply sit with you in your pain. These are your safe people. The ones who don't tell you how to grieve but instead allow you to be exactly where you are. Maybe it's the friend who shows up without expectation, the family member who quietly checks in, or the therapist who helps you make sense of the mess inside. Seek out those who bring comfort, not pressure.

Let Connection Be on Your Terms

Stepping back into the world after a loss is not an all-or-nothing process. You don't have to dive headfirst into social gatherings, force small talk, or pretend to be okay when you're not. Start small. Maybe it's answering a text instead of ignoring it. Maybe it's accepting a hug instead of shrinking away. Maybe it's taking a walk with a friend. Connection doesn't have to be big to be meaningful. Even the smallest moments of shared presence can remind you that you are not as alone as grief may make you feel.

Trust That Your Pain Deserves to Be Seen

Grief can make you feel invisible. People around you continue with their lives, and it's easy to wonder if your loss even registers to them the way it does to you. But your grief matters because your love matters. Hiding it won't make it disappear—it only makes it heavier to carry. You don't have to share your grief with the world but find spaces where it can exist without shame. Maybe that's through writing, through therapy, through speaking their name aloud. However, you choose to express it and allow your pain to be acknowledged, even if only by yourself at first.

One of the first steps I took back into the world was a weekly hike with my best friend and a group of other women. I brought my dog, Pepper, and for the first time in what felt like forever, I could breathe. The open sky, the steady rhythm of my feet on the trail, the expansive oak trees, the quiet understanding of those around me—it all reminded me that I was still here. My best friend later shared with me that one of the women had hesitated to come on the walks at first, afraid she wouldn't know what to say to me. My friend reassured her: *Just treat her as you always have. She speaks Jenna's name openly. She welcomes you remembering her.*

That simple truth—that I wanted Jenna's name spoken, that I needed to keep her memory alive—became a bridge between me and the world I no longer knew how to exist in. And having a friend who gently helped me re-engage, who advocated for what I needed when I wasn't always sure how to ask for it, made all the difference.

Taking that first step toward connection—whether it's a walk, a phone call, or simply allowing someone to sit beside you can feel too much effort. But slowly, in small and deliberate ways, re-engaging with the world can soften the weight of isolation. It is in these moments of reaching out that love begins to move again—not as a replacement for your loss, but as a bridge back to life.

WHY LETTING PEOPLE IN MATTERS

Grief has a way of convincing us that no one else could possibly understand the depth of our pain. It whispers that retreating inward is safer, that the world beyond our grief is too distant, too unrecognizable to step into. But in truth, allowing others in—bit by bit, at our own pace—is not about forcing healing. It is about making space for love to exist alongside the pain.

LETTING PEOPLE IN

The days after Jenna's passing were filled with an overwhelming influx of people, family, friends, neighbors, and even strangers—showing up at our door. At times, the steady stream of visitors felt too much to bear. I wanted to close the door and retreat from the world, but deep down, I understood the significance of letting people in.

One afternoon, a woman from our neighborhood, someone I barely knew, arrived unannounced with a casserole in her hands. She looked hesitant, unsure of whether she should stay or leave. I stood at the door, paralyzed by conflicting emotions. Part of me wanted to tell her I couldn't handle another interaction. But then I realized that closing the door on her might mean shutting out the love she was offering—something I desperately needed, even if I didn't fully understand it at the moment.

I opened the door wider and invited her in. She placed the dish on the counter and gave me a tight hug. "I'm here for you, whatever you need," she said. Her words weren't grand or profound, but they grounded me in a way I didn't expect. That moment was a small but significant reminder that even amidst the chaos of grief, the love and kindness of others could be the much-needed wind beneath my wings.

Letting people in doesn't mean engaging with everyone all the time, nor does it mean talking when you're not ready. It simply means allowing yourself to be witnessed in your grief—to have your pain honored by the presence of another.

GRIEF AND THE WALLS WE BUILD: HOW ONE FRIEND'S PRESENCE MADE A DIFFERENCE

Through my work with #hersmile, I've had the privilege of hearing countless stories of love, loss, and resilience. One that has stayed with me is Rachel's.

Rachel lost her younger brother in a sudden car accident. They were only two years apart, inseparable since childhood, and their bond extended into every part of their lives. They shared the same circle of friends, the same late-night conversations, the same memories that no one else could quite understand. To everyone who knew them, Rachel and her brother weren't just siblings, they were the heart of their group, the glue that kept their friends connected.

And then, just like that, he was gone.

After his passing, Rachel withdrew. The once-lively friend group that had always revolved around her and her brother suddenly felt fractured. Calls and texts went unanswered. Friends who had always felt close to her now felt like strangers standing on the outside of a pain they didn't know how to reach. No one knew what to say or how to help, and Rachel, drowning in grief, didn't know how to let them in.

One night, one of her friends, Sarah, decided to show up at Rachel's house. She hesitated at the door, unsure if she was making the right choice. But she knocked anyway.

Rachel answered, her eyes hollow with exhaustion. Sarah didn't try to fill the silence with forced words or empty reassurances. She simply stepped inside and sat next to her on the couch.

For a long time, they sat there quietly, the weight of absence filling the space between them. Then, finally, Rachel whispered, *"I don't know how to do this without him."*

Sarah just nodded and hugged her. And in that simple gesture, a small crack formed in the isolation Rachel had wrapped herself in.

Sarah didn't fix Rachel's grief that night. But she reminded her that she didn't have to carry it alone.

This is the power of showing up. Grief is isolating, but connection—just sitting beside someone in their pain—can soften its sharpest edges. Sometimes, it's about allowing someone to sit with you in your pain—to hold even a fraction of it, for even a fraction of a moment.

FOR A MOMENT, SHE WAS HERE AGAIN: THE HEALING GIFT OF SHARED STORIES

Another story that stands out and was shared with me was by a woman named Lisa, who lost her best friend to cancer.

In the early days after her passing, Lisa found herself caught in a cycle of guilt. Every time she smiled, every time she caught herself enjoying even the smallest moment, it felt like a betrayal. *How could I still feel joy when she was gone?* she had wondered. The weight of that question kept her distant, detached from the people who loved her. She stopped going out, withdrew from conversations, and avoided places that once brought comfort.

Then, one afternoon, a group of coworkers convinced her to join them at a café. She sat quietly, sipping her iced vanilla coffee latte, not quite present. But then, someone brought up the time her best friend had got them all lost on a road trip, and suddenly, the entire table was laughing.

Lisa hesitated. And then, before she could stop herself, she smiled—a real, genuine smile.

Later, she told me, *"For a moment, it was like she was here again."*

That's what sharing stories does. It breathes life into the love that remains. It reminds us that our person is not only in the past—they are still woven into who we are now. The presence of others, especially those who knew and loved the one we lost, can create a bridge between grief and connection, between sorrow and solace. In sharing stories, they don't just remember with us—they breathe life into the precious memories we're afraid of losing, reminding us that love endures time and place.

Even in early grief, when laughter feels impossible, there may come a moment—unexpected, fleeting—where love finds a way through. And in those moments, we remember that grief and joy are not opposites. They can exist together, side by side, each honoring the love that never fades.

HOW A SHOVELED DRIVEWAY OPENED THE DOOR TO HEALING

Another story I heard through my work with #hersmile was from a man named James. His wife had passed suddenly, and in the days and weeks that followed, he did what so many grieving people do—he withdrew. He insisted he was fine. He turned down offers for meals, ignored invitations, and kept his grief locked inside. People who cared about him wanted to help, but he wouldn't let them in. It wasn't that he didn't appreciate their concern, he just didn't know how to receive it.

Then, one winter morning, after a heavy snowstorm, James opened his front door to find his driveway already shoveled. No one had knocked. No one had asked for a thank you. Someone had simply shown up for him in the quietest of ways.

Later that day, he learned it was his next-door neighbor, Tom, who had done it. Tom had lost his own wife years before and knew, in ways others couldn't, how isolating grief could be. He hadn't asked

James what he needed, he had just done something, offering his presence without expectation.

That small, quiet act sat with James. A few days later, for the first time in months, he walked over to Tom's house. He didn't go with the intention of talking about his grief—he wasn't sure he even could. But as they stood in the doorway, James found himself sharing a story about his wife, the kind of small, beautiful memory that people don't often share unless they feel safe.

If you are in the depths of grief, I know how hard it can be to open that door—even just a little. But when we let in even the smallest light, we create space not only for support but for a deeper kind of healing—one that acknowledges that grief does not exist in isolation.

The love that surrounds you, when you are ready to receive it, can be a steadying hand, a warm meal, a quiet presence in the silence. And in time, it may be the very thing that helps you carry your love forward into the world again.

PRACTICAL WAYS TO LET OTHERS IN

While the idea of connection may feel overwhelming, small, intentional steps can make a difference:

- **Accept Help Graciously** – Allowing others to assist with tasks like preparing meals, cleaning, picking up groceries, or even humbly accepting cash donations can alleviate some of the stress you may not even realize you're carrying. Accepting help is not a sign of weakness, it's a step toward healing.
- **Create Boundaries** – Letting people in doesn't mean you need to engage with everyone all the time. It's okay to set boundaries and let others know when you need time to

yourself. A trusted friend or family member can help manage interactions, so you don't feel overwhelmed.

- **Be Honest About Your Needs** – If you're comfortable, share what you need most with your support network. Whether it's someone to sit quietly with you, someone to babysit the kids, watch your pets, help with daily responsibilities, or simply check in via text, communicating your needs allows others to support you in meaningful ways.

The steps we take out of isolation are often small, tentative, and uncertain. Yet, through small acts—accepting help, setting boundaries, and expressing our needs—we slowly begin to reassimilate into life, not as it was, but as it is now.

FINAL REFLECTION

In the rawest moments of early grief, survival is the only goal. There is no roadmap, no step-by-step guide to navigate the impossible. And yet, as the days turn into weeks, and the weight of loss shifts— sometimes crushing, sometimes numbing—a quiet truth begins to emerge: grief is not just something we endure; it is something we are asked to live with.

At first, that weight feels unbearable. It feels like something that will break us. And in some ways, it does. But in time, we come to see that grief is not just a reflection of loss, it is a reflection of love. And love does not disappear. It changes, it reshapes itself, and it finds new ways to exist.

Slowly, we take steps—small ones at first—out of isolation. We allow others to witness our pain, not to fix it, but simply to hold space for it. We learn to interact with our grief rather than be consumed by it. We discover that even in the deepest sorrow, there are moments of connection, moments where love reaches through the darkness and reminds us that we are not alone.

Grief does not ask us to let go. It asks us to integrate. To take what we have lost and weave it into the life we still have. To carry our love forward, not in place of the pain, but alongside it.

And so, as you stand at the edge of this new reality—this before and after you never asked for—know this: you do not have to have it all figured out. You do not have to rush. You do not have to force meaning or healing before you are ready.

All you have to do is take the next step. However small, however uncertain.

Grief will walk with you. But so will love. And in time, love will be what carries you forward.

3
EXPRESSING GRIEF AND COMMUNICATING NEEDS

I wanted to show my girls and husband that we could do this—somehow, some way—we could get through this. So keeping it all together was something I couldn't risk getting wrong.

One quiet evening, I sat on the back deck, the sky ablaze with hues of orange and pink as the sun dipped below my roofline. A warm breeze stirred the trees, rustling the leaves in a gentle whisper as if the world itself was speaking in hushed tones around my grief. The scent of jasmine drifted through the air, bittersweet in its beauty, much like the moment itself. It was almost unbearable, a sharp contrast to the weight pressing on my chest, a weight I had carried for so long it had become part of me.

I had grown so used to holding my grief in silence, clutching it tightly as though it were the last thread connecting me to Jenna. It wasn't just sorrow I was protecting; it was myself. Letting people in felt dangerous, like stepping too close to an open wound. I didn't want to see their sadness for me reflected in their eyes, the way their gazes softened, their words slowed, as if I might break beneath the weight of their sympathy. I didn't want their well-meaning phrases

*—She's always with you, time will help, you're so strong—*to cut deeper into wounds that were already raw.

And yet, in that quiet space between day and night, as I stared at the sky painted in impossible colors, a thought brushed against me, fleeting but insistent: *What if holding it all together wasn't the only way forward?*

I feared that people's pity, their sorrow, might make the weight of it all even harder to bear. And more than anything, I was terrified that speaking my pain aloud would somehow dim the light of the only thing that mattered to me—the love I had for Jenna. Communicating the depth of my sadness, the anger, the disappointment, and the overwhelming lack of control felt like it might reduce that love to something smaller, something I couldn't risk losing. So I stayed silent, locking those emotions inside, convincing myself that silence was strength, that holding it all in was my way of honoring her.

So, as the vibrant colors faded into the stillness of dusk, a quiet truth settled over me—one that both unsettled and freed me: I wasn't just holding my grief—I was afraid to let it breathe. Afraid that if I gave it space, it might take over completely, leaving nothing behind but emptiness. I realized, sitting there alone with the rustle of leaves as my only company, that this silence wasn't serving me. It wasn't protecting me; it was isolating me.

That evening, I allowed myself to exhale. For the first time, I let the emotions I had been holding back rise to the surface—unfiltered and raw. The tears came, not as a surrender, but as a release. And in that moment, I understood something I hadn't let myself believe before: expressing my grief wasn't a betrayal of my love for Jenna. It was a testament to it. Every tear, every pang of sadness, every moment of raw vulnerability was a reflection of the love that would always live inside me.

Letting those feelings out didn't make the pain disappear, but it lightened the weight I was carrying, even if just a little. I began to see that my silence wasn't protecting my love, it was shielding me from the connection I so desperately needed. By giving my emotions room to breathe, I was able to connect more deeply—not just with my ongoing relationship with Jenna, but with my younger daughters, my husband, and the people who cared about me.

Learning to carry the pain that comes with grief isn't easy. And sometimes, the bravest thing we can do is to let the pain breathe. To let the sorrow, the anger, and the tenderness rise to the surface. To trust that our hearts are strong enough to hold it all—the weight of loss and the beauty of love—without diminishing either.

TUNING INTO YOUR FEELINGS: THE PATH TO EMOTIONAL AWARENESS

In these moments of stillness, you may find yourself face-to-face with a kaleidoscope of emotions—sadness, anger, guilt, confusion, and, if only fleeting, moments of calm. It's human to feel a bit detached when the full weight of your emotions presses in, but giving yourself permission to explore them, one at a time, is an act of courage, in my opinion. Start small. Name what you're feeling, even if it's just a whisper to yourself or a scribble on a page. Writing it down or saying it aloud transforms the intangible into something real—something you can sit with, examine, and eventually make sense of.

Dr. Alan Wolfelt, a trusted voice in understanding grief, reminds us that naming and sharing these emotions, whether on paper, in conversation, or in quiet reflection—is an invitation to healing. Vulnerability doesn't erase pain, but it opens the door to awareness. By acknowledging what you're feeling, you create space to process it, to be seen in your humanity, and to ease some of the isolation that grief can bring. Grief has a way of knotting us up inside, making our unspoken feelings weigh heavier with each passing day. But when you name and express those emotions—let's be honest, sometimes calling grief exactly what it feels like (a total bitch)—you loosen that knot, giving your heart and mind the space they need to breathe and allowing healing to gently take root.

There will come a moment—and maybe it hasn't happened yet—when you'll face the daunting task of sitting quietly with your emotions. For many, this might feel impossible or deeply uncomfortable. After all, who wants to willingly sit with emotional pain? The fear of being consumed by it can feel so real, especially if you've been taught to "suck it up" or push through life's hardships without pause. Holding everything tightly often feels safer, like a way to keep yourself together when the ground beneath you has already crumbled. Letting go, even slightly, can feel terrifying, as if grief might overwhelm your psyche entirely. Yet expressing your emotions isn't about losing control, it's about creating that vital space to release what's been held in your heart, twisted in your stomach, or spinning endlessly in your mind. Many of us weren't taught how to navigate our feelings, often growing up in environments where we were encouraged to "stay strong" or "don't cry." So it's no wonder that sitting with emotions can feel foreign or even frightening.

If this is where you find yourself, know I understand, and there is no judgment in how difficult this might feel. Sitting with your emotions isn't about flipping a switch and suddenly being okay with discomfort. You've already been through so much. This is more like cracking open a door and peeking in, letting just a sliver of light come through—not in the sense of fixing or solving—but gently asking, *What is this feeling trying to tell me?* Start small. Maybe it's just a single moment of acknowledgment, a fleeting pause to notice what's stirring inside you. That's enough.

And if curiosity feels out of reach, that's okay too. This process takes time, and it's important to meet yourself exactly where you are. You don't need to force yourself to sit in the depths of your pain all at once, nor to the depths you will ever need to go. Instead, think of it as dipping your toe into the water, acknowledging just one feeling, one breath, one moment at a time. It might feel like fear or overwhelm at first, but over time, those feelings begin to shift, even if just slightly.

When you allow yourself to gently experience your emotions, you'll start to notice that they don't hold the same power to consume you. They're not here to stay forever; they're visitors passing through should you offer them an exit door, and by letting them come and go, you take the first steps toward healing. This doesn't mean the pain completely disappears—it doesn't—but it begins to transform. It becomes something you can live with, something less sharp, less overwhelming.

This journey is also not about being fearless or perfect, it's about finding compassion for yourself in every small step forward. If sitting with your emotions feels too much today, give yourself grace. If curiosity feels inaccessible, that's okay too. It takes time, patience, and tenderness to learn how to navigate emotions, especially when, as I said, many of us were never taught how. And in the moments when it feels impossible, remind yourself that simply being willing to try—to even consider being with your emotions for one moment —is an act of courage in itself. Resilience doesn't come from never falling; it comes from giving yourself grace as you learn to rise.

And grief can be winding and unpredictable. Some weeks it may feel like you're taking two steps forward and one step back. Some days, the light will feel warm on your face, and on others, the clouds will roll in, leaving you questioning if you've made any progress at all. Again, give yourself compassion. The important thing is to stay attuned to your emotions, to acknowledge their presence without letting them pull you under. For me, I like to imagine opening a door in my mind for my emotions to enter—a quiet invitation to let them visit. It's taken me time to learn how to do this, but I now sit with them for a moment, notice them, and let them tell me what they need to say. And when it feels right, I open another door in my mind for them to pass through and leave. This visual aid helps me set the intention of emotional movement—allowing the feelings to flow, instead of getting stuck. It's a gentle reminder: *Okay, you came, you visited, and now it's time to go.* By tuning in this way, you'll begin to find moments of balance amidst the emotional waves.

For me, it's a humble reminder that this is the greatest form of control we can have—to stay connected to our own emotional land-scape, even when it feels messy and overwhelming. It's about allowing yourself to gently notice what emotions are showing up and handing out the strongest directives. These moments, no matter how small, remind you that you're stronger and braver than you know.

REFLECTION EXERCISE: EMOTIONAL CHECK-IN

Here's a short list of questions and follow-up prompts to help you name and explore your emotions, step by step. These are designed to guide you gently, offering clarity and space for self-reflection:

1. **What am I feeling right now?**

   - Start with the basics: *Am I sad, angry, confused, or overwhelmed? Do I feel calm or hopeful?*
   - Don't overanalyze, just name the first thing that comes to mind, even if it feels unclear or incomplete.

2. **Where do I feel this emotion in my body?**

   - Ask yourself: *Do I feel tightness in my chest? A knot in my stomach? Heaviness in my limbs?*

- Connecting physical sensations to your emotions can make them feel more tangible and less overwhelming.

3. What triggered this feeling?

- Explore: *Did something happen today that brought this up? Was it a memory, a conversation, or simply the quiet of the moment?*
- Acknowledge the source without judgment—it could be big or small.

4. What does this emotion need from me?

- Reflect: *Do I need to sit with this for a moment, cry, write it down, or share it with someone?*
- Ask yourself what might help ease or honor the feeling, even in a small way.

5. Is there another layer to this feeling?

- Go deeper: *Am I angry, or is there sadness underneath? Am I feeling guilt, or is it tied to love and regret?*
- Emotions often come in layers; naming them can help you peel back each one with care.

6. What would I say to a friend feeling this way?

- Consider: *If someone I cared about was experiencing this emotion, what would I tell them? What compassion or advice would I offer?*
- Often, the kindness we extend to others is the kindness we need for ourselves.

Example Flow:

- *What am I feeling right now?* → "I feel overwhelmed."
- *Where do I feel it in my body?* → "There's a tightness in my chest."
- *What triggered this feeling?* → "I saw a picture of Jenna today, and it brought back so many precious memories."
- *What does this emotion need from me?* → "I think I need to take some deep breaths and let myself just cry."
- *Is there another layer to this feeling?* → "Maybe I'm not just overwhelmed—I'm sad because I miss her so much, and I feel such a void in my heart."

By using these questions, you're giving yourself permission to pause, reflect, and give your emotions the space they need to exist, be acknowledged, and be validated. This is about showing up for yourself, moment by moment.

BLENDING PERSONAL AND CULTURAL NEEDS IN COMMUNICATION

Tapping into your emotions and becoming more aware of them can be transformative, but it's not always straightforward. What you allow yourself to feel or even recognize can be deeply influenced by cultural norms and expectations. This interplay between personal grief and cultural expectations often requires reflection and, at times, a willingness to challenge ingrained beliefs—an act that is far from easy. Cultural norms are often so deeply woven into our identities that we may not even recognize how they shape our emotional responses. They can tell us what is "acceptable" to feel, how we're supposed to grieve, or what roles we must fulfill, even when those roles can add to our pain.

But how do you begin to question what feels so fundamental to who you are? Start by tuning into your emotional and physical responses. Are you experiencing guilt, shame, or anger that feels disproportionate or all-encompassing? Are you carrying tension in your body —tightness in your chest, a knot in your stomach, or a heaviness in your shoulders—that never seems to ease no matter the months or years that pass by? These can be signs that your emotional needs are not being met, that the way you've been taught to process your emotions might be adding to your burden rather than helping you heal.

The first step is curiosity. Ask yourself: Does this belief serve me, or is it keeping me stuck? Is this guilt or expectation something I truly believe, or something I've been taught to carry? Would I extend the same judgment or expectation to someone I love? It takes incredible bravery to even consider that there may be a healthier, more compassionate way to process your emotions, especially when it feels like questioning your cultural foundation is questioning your very identity. This can create a profound sense of vulnerability, as if letting go of certain beliefs or traditions is yet another form of loss— a death of something deeply ingrained within you. But what if, instead of seeing it as a loss, you viewed it as an evolution? Deepening your relationship with yourself doesn't have to mean abandoning your culture; it can mean engaging with it in a new and more meaningful way.

Every relationship, whether with others, with your culture, or with yourself, becomes richer and more fulfilling when it's approached relationally—when there's space for growth, understanding, and adaptation. By exploring your emotions with curiosity and compassion, you're not rejecting your customs. You're building a bridge between the values you hold dear and the person you're becoming. This process can honor both your individuality and the traditions that have shaped you, allowing you to carry them forward in a way that's authentic to your healing journey.

ARASH'S PATH: NAVIGATING GRIEF AT THE CROSSROADS OF TRADITION AND HEALING

Arash was born in a small village in northern Iran, where the teachings of his culture were as enduring as the mountains surrounding his home. Stoicism was a value passed down through generations—fathers were expected to be steadfast protectors, silent pillars of strength who shielded their families from hardship. Emotions were to be carried inward, not worn on the sleeve. This is the way it had always been, and for much of his childhood, Arash embraced this identity without question.

But when Arash was 17, his family moved to the United States in pursuit of better opportunities. The transition was both exciting and unsettling, thrusting him into a world where cultural norms were markedly different. In this new environment, Arash encountered ideas that challenged the stoicism he had been taught to revere. Friends spoke openly about their feelings, and teachers encouraged self-reflection and dialogue. While he never stopped honoring the values of his upbringing, Arash couldn't deny the positive influence these new perspectives had on his worldview. They planted seeds of curiosity and a willingness to consider that strength could take many forms.

Years later, as an adult living in California, Arash's stoic foundation was tested in a way he could have never imagined. His six-year-old son, Kian, was diagnosed with an aggressive form of leukemia. Arash's role as protector was one, he had taken deeply to heart, and the diagnosis shattered him. He threw himself into the fight, seeking out specialists, researching every possible treatment, and working tirelessly to save his boy. But despite his efforts, the illness progressed. When Kian passed away, Arash was left with an overwhelming sense of failure. His identity as a father—rooted in his ability to protect—seemed to crumble beneath him.

The guilt was suffocating. Arash replayed every decision, questioning whether he had done enough, wondering if he had missed something that could have saved his son. Adding to his pain was the cultural weight he carried: in his Iranian upbringing, a father's strength and control were non-negotiable. To show vulnerability, let alone seek help, felt like an admission of defeat. He retreated inward, avoiding friends, family, and even his wife. The weight of his silence began to isolate him further.

One evening, Arash attended a remembrance service for children lost to illness, organized by a local community center. It was here that the cultural influences of his upbringing and his life in the United States began to merge in a meaningful way. An Iranian elder shared a poem by Rumi about grief being the wound through which light enters. The elder spoke of how mourning is not a betrayal of strength but an act of love. Another speaker, an American therapist, shared practical insights on how to navigate grief by naming emotions and leaning into community support. The combination of these teachings resonated deeply with Arash, offering him permission to acknowledge his pain without judgment.

Encouraged by what he heard, Arash began seeking help in small, manageable ways. He started attending a multicultural grief support group where individuals from diverse backgrounds shared their stories. Listening to others speak openly about their struggles helped him feel less alone. For the first time, he considered that his grief wasn't a failure but a natural response to the immense love he held for Kian.

Accepting help didn't come easily. Arash had to confront deeply ingrained beliefs about what it meant to be a father and a man. He began journaling, something he had learned about from one of the support group facilitators. At first, his writing felt stilted and awkward, but gradually, it became a space where he could untangle the complexity of his emotions. He wrote about the guilt that weighed on him, the anger he felt toward the universe, and the unbearable ache of missing his son. Through these pages, Arash began to understand that expressing his emotions didn't diminish his strength—it deepened it.

He also leaned into his cultural traditions in new ways. He began visiting Kian's grave weekly, bringing small offerings of flowers and lighting candles, as was customary in his Iranian heritage. But he paired these visits with something he had learned from his new life in America: mindfulness. Sitting quietly by the gravesite, he would focus on his breath, allowing his emotions to rise and fall like waves. This blending of traditions—honoring his cultural roots while embracing new practices—helped him find balance.

Over time, Arash realized that the teachings of his childhood and the insights he had gained in the United States were not at odds; they were complementary. His Iranian upbringing had given him resilience and a deep sense of responsibility, while the openness he encountered in American culture showed him strength in vulnerability. Together, they formed a meaningful path forward.

One of the most profound moments came during a Persian New Year celebration, where Arash shared a poem by Rumi with his grief support group. *"Try not to resist the changes that come your way,"* he read aloud. *"Instead, let life live through you. And do not worry that your life is turning upside down. How do you know that the side you are used to is better than the one to come?"* After reading the poem, he shared his story with the group, something he had never done before. The act of speaking his truth out loud—naming his guilt, his love, and his grief —felt like a release. The group's warmth and understanding filled him with the renewal that love brings.

Arash's journey is not easy, but it has been transformative. He has learned that grief doesn't have to be borne in silence, and that strength comes in many forms. By blending the stoic resilience of his Iranian roots with the emotional openness he has encountered in the

United States, Arash has found a way to honor both his heritage and his heart. His story reminds us that healing often requires us to look beyond what we've always known, to embrace the wisdom of multiple perspectives, and to allow ourselves the grace to grieve in ways that feel authentic to who we are.

Finally, this willingness to reflect and question isn't about rejecting your culture—it's about finding balance. It's about recognizing that you can honor your customs while also allowing yourself the space to explore what truly supports your healing. In this intersection of the personal and the cultural lies the opportunity to not only grow as an individual but also redefine how you move through grief in a way that is both authentic and deeply respectful of where you come from.

SEEKING SUPPORT

Reaching out for support can feel daunting when you're consumed by grief, yet it's one of the boldest steps you can take. In my own experience, I learned the hard way just how important—and complicated—it can be to express your needs. About six months after Jenna passed, I found myself growing increasingly angry with one of my closest friends. Weeks would go by without her calling, and when we did talk, the conversations stayed surface-level. She'd ask, "How are you?" and I'd automatically say, "I'm fine." And that was it. Small talk would follow, while resentment continued to build.

I wanted her to dig deeper. I longed for her to say, "No, really—how are you? I'm here for you. You're not alone." But she never went there. I felt abandoned, convinced she didn't care enough to jump into the hole with me. Eventually, my frustration reached a boiling point, and I told her how I felt—that she wasn't there for me, that she wasn't really listening or showing up.

Her response shocked me. She said, "When I ask how you're doing, and you say 'fine,' I assume you don't want to talk about it. I didn't want to upset you more by pushing."

That moment shifted my perspective. She wasn't being neglectful or indifferent; she was doing her best with the information she had. She didn't want to cross a boundary I hadn't clearly set. This realization was humbling—it reminded me that people often don't know what the "right" thing to do is when we're grieving. Most don't want to make things worse, so they tread lightly, often waiting for a signal from us.

This is why expressing our needs is so vital, even though it can feel vulnerable and exhausting. Grief already asks so much of us, and the idea of having to guide others in how to support us might feel unfair. I know it felt very unfair to me. But articulating what we need—whether it's a listening ear, help with something, or just someone digging a little deeper—can help lighten some of the burdens we're carrying.

You might start with something as simple as, *"I'm feeling over-whelmed and need someone to talk to. Could we chat for a bit?"* or *"Would you mind spending time with me? I don't need advice—just your presence."* If you're struggling with daily responsibilities, it can help to be specific: *"I've been having a hard time keeping up with meals. Could you help me cook dinner or drop off something?"* Clarity doesn't burden others; it empowers them to show up in a way that's truly helpful.

And when people do show up for you, expressing gratitude can deepen those bonds. Saying something like, "I'm so thankful you're here for me—your support means more than I can say," creates a shared understanding and encourages them to stay present. Most people want to help; they're just afraid of doing the wrong thing. By guiding them, you create a bridge of care that benefits everyone involved.

In those moments when it feels unfair to have to ask, remember this: seeking support is a way of honoring your own needs and allowing others to show up for you in meaningful ways. It's about allowing others to walk alongside you, sharing the weight of your grief. It's also about giving them the opportunity to love you in the best way they can. Yes, it requires vulnerability, especially if you've been conditioned to "suck it up" or bear your pain in silence. But when you allow yourself to be vulnerable, you create space for healing—not just for yourself but for those who care about you.

Grief is an imperfect dance. You're learning to communicate your needs in a world that often struggles to understand the depth of your loss and pain. Be patient with yourself and others. Expressing your needs, as hard as it may feel, is a gift—to you, to your support network, and to the love that still connects you to the person who is no longer physically here.

If, after expressing your needs, someone still doesn't show up for you, it can feel like another layer of grief—a loss within a loss. It's painful to feel unheard or unsupported, especially when you've already forced yourself to open up and communicate your needs. In these moments, it's important to remember a few key things:

1. **It's Not About You**: Often, when people can't meet us in our grief, it has more to do with their own limitations than anything we've done. They may be overwhelmed, unsure of what to say, or struggling with their own unresolved emotions. This doesn't excuse their absence, but it can help to remind yourself that their inability to show up isn't a reflection of your worth or how much you are loved.

2. **Release Expectations**: Holding onto expectations of how others should behave can compound your pain. It's natural to want people to instinctively know what you need, but the truth is, not everyone can or is willing to jump in the hole with us. Releasing those expectations doesn't mean you

stop hoping for connection—it means you free yourself from the weight of disappointment when others fall short.

3. **Set Boundaries to Protect Your Energy**: If someone consistently falls short in offering support, it's okay to release your expectations with love and create some distance. This isn't about blame or punishment—it's about honoring your emotional well-being. You can still hold care and compassion for them while recognizing that they may not be the person you can lean on during this chapter of your life.

4. **Turn Toward Those Who Do Show Up**: Shift your focus to the people who are present and willing to walk alongside you. It may not be the person you expected, but meaningful support often comes from unexpected places. It may truly amaze you. I know it amazed me.

5. **Practice Forgiveness—for Yourself and Others**: When feelings of anger, disappointment, or resentment arise toward someone who hasn't shown up for you, allow yourself to fully experience those emotions. Let them move through you without judgment or resistance. Awareness is the first step in healing. Over time, consider opening your heart to forgiveness—not to condone their actions, but to release yourself from the emotional weight they carry. Likewise, offer yourself grace if forgiveness doesn't come easily. Healing is a journey, and every emotion you allow to flow through you brings you closer to peace.

6. **Honor Your Needs**: If you're feeling unsupported, turn inward and ask yourself what you can do to nurture your own well-being. This might mean journaling, seeking professional guidance, or exploring new avenues of connection, such as support groups. Remind yourself that your needs matter, and it's okay to prioritize them.

When Jenna passed away, several casual friends rushed to our side, stepping into the darkest, most intimate part of my life without hesitation. Their support left a lasting legacy. Yet, one individual, despite all she did for our family, brought greater emotional challenges into my life. While I was grateful for her help, her frequent drama and personal despair left me emotionally drained and conflicted.

I remembered a friend once sharing that she released her ex-husband and their marriage with love, and they remained friends after the divorce. That beautiful intention stayed with me, and I was determined to approach my own challenging relationship with the same grace. It took two years to let go, but I did so with love as my guide. And, perhaps, the best part of this story is we remain casual friends to this day.

This experience taught me that forgiveness isn't about excusing harmful and self-serving behaviors; it's about freeing yourself from their hold. Over time, consider opening your heart to forgiveness, both for others and for yourself. Healing is a journey, and every emotion you allow to flow through you brings you closer to peace. Moving forward when someone doesn't show up for you in the way that serves you involves accepting their limitations while honoring your own needs. Remember, you can love people from afar while prioritizing your own well-being. Releasing the pain tied to unmet expectations creates space for the love and support that does exist to grow.

Above all, remember this: your grief is valid, and your needs are important. Not everyone will have the capacity to meet you in your pain, and some people will try to make their pain greater than yours, but that doesn't diminish the value of what you're feeling or what you need.

Be gentle with yourself as you navigate these moments and know that finding the right support is an essential part of your healing journey. Like shedding a heavy coat no longer needed in warmer weather, consider releasing relationships that no longer serve your healing, allowing forgiveness and love to guide you forward.

EXPRESSING GRIEF AND COMMUNICATING NEEDS AFTER A SUICIDE LOSS

For those navigating the grief of losing someone to suicide, the weight of expressing your pain and communicating your needs can feel deeply conflicting. It's a type of grief that often feels isolating, tangled with unspoken questions, unrelenting guilt, and a deep sense of helplessness. In this kind of loss, asking for support can feel almost impossible—how could your distress even begin to matter compared to the pain your loved one must have endured? The thought of voicing your needs may feel selfish or insignificant, as though prioritizing your own emotions diminishes the gravity of what happened.

But here's the truth: your grief and your needs are not in competition with the loss you've experienced. They coexist, intertwined, in a way that reflects the complexity of your love and your pain. Caring for your emotional well-being doesn't diminish the depth of your sorrow or the profound respect you hold for the emotional struggles your loved one endured. Instead, it's a vital part of the healing process, a way to begin untangling the knot of emotions that come with the complexities of suicide.

But what do you do when you need help, but you're not ready to talk about the details of your loved one's passing? How can you seek support while setting boundaries about what you're ready—or not ready—to share? These are challenging questions, and they reflect the layers of grieving a loss by suicide. If you find yourself grappling with these emotions, know that it's natural. It's okay to protect your heart while still seeking the care and connection you need. Here are some strategies to help you navigate this delicate balance:

1. Set Clear Boundaries About What You're Ready to Share

It's only human for others to have questions about your loved one's death, but you don't owe anyone an explanation. It's okay to communicate that you're not ready—or willing—to discuss certain details. For example, you could say:

- "I'm not ready to talk about the details of what happened, but I appreciate you talking with me."
- "Right now, it's too painful for me to go into specifics, but I'd love to talk about how I'm feeling or memories I have of [their name]."

These responses gently redirect the conversation while preserving your boundaries. Most people will understand and respect this if you're honest about your limits.

2. Find Support in Safe Spaces

If discussing your loss feels too much, consider starting with spaces specifically designed for grief support, such as a counselor, therapist, or a suicide loss support group. These environments are typically more attuned to the complexities of suicide-related grief, offering a level of understanding and safety that can help you begin to process your emotions without judgment or pressure to share more than you're ready to.

For example:

- Seek out a therapist who specializes in grief or suicide loss. They can help you navigate your feelings while respecting your boundaries.
- Join a support group for suicide loss survivors. Hearing others share their stories may help you feel less alone while also giving you permission to share at your own pace.

3. Prepare Responses for Uncomfortable Questions

Unfortunately, not everyone knows how to navigate conversations around grief, especially after a suicide. People may ask invasive or insensitive questions, even if they have good intentions. Preparing responses ahead of time can help you feel more in control when these moments arise. Consider using phrases like:

- "That's not something I'm ready to talk about right now but thank you for caring."
- "I appreciate your concern, but I'm focusing on healing and remembering the good times with [their name]."
- "I'd rather not get into the details—it's too painful for me."

Having these responses at the ready can ease the stress of feeling caught off guard.

4. Communicate Your Needs to Close Friends and Family

If you feel comfortable, let your inner circle know how they can best support you. For example:

- Tell them you'd prefer it if they focused on how they can help you day-to-day instead of asking questions about the circumstances of the loss.
- Share that simply sitting with you, listening, or offering practical help like cooking or errands means more than any words they could say.

This clarity helps the people closest to you avoid unintentional missteps while showing them that their presence matters.

5. Acknowledge the Emotional Complexity of Boundaries

Setting boundaries can bring up its own set of emotions, such as guilt or fear of judgment. Remind yourself that protecting your well-being doesn't diminish the respect or love you have for the person you've lost. It's okay to prioritize your healing by creating space between you and conversations that feel too heavy or invasive.

You might say to yourself:

- "My grief is valid, and I don't need to justify it by sharing details I'm not ready to talk about."
- "It's okay to focus on what helps me heal right now. This doesn't make me selfish—it makes me human."

6. Use Alternative Ways to Honor and Express Your Grief

If verbalizing your feelings feels too overwhelming, explore other outlets for your grief. Writing letters to your loved one, creating art, or even taking quiet walks can help you process your emotions without needing to explain them to anyone else. These private acts of expression allow you to honor your loss in ways that feel authentic and safe.

7. Let Go of Unrealistic Expectations

It's important to release the idea that you need to have all the answers or be "strong" in the way others might expect. Grieving after a suicide is an intensely personal and complicated experience. It's okay to move at your own pace, to share when you're ready, and to hold back when you're not. Remind yourself that your journey is valid, no matter how it unfolds.

8. Find a Trusted Advocate

If navigating these conversations feels like it's too much, consider asking a trusted friend or family member to act as a buffer. They can explain to others what you're comfortable sharing, sparing you from having to repeat the same explanations or set boundaries with multiple people.

9. Practice Self-Compassion

Above all, be gentle with yourself. It's okay to feel conflicted, to need space, and to struggle with finding the words to express what you're going through. Remind yourself that you are worthy of support, even if it takes time to figure out how to receive it.

Navigating grief after suicide is deeply complex, and the need to protect yourself while seeking support can feel like a delicate balancing act. By setting clear boundaries, finding safe spaces, and exploring alternative ways to process your emotions, you can create a framework that honors both your grief and your healing. It's not about shutting people out or avoiding the pain, it's about giving yourself the time and space to heal in a way that feels right for you. Above all, know this: you are not alone, and you deserve care, compassion, and connection on this journey.

DECLINING OFFERS OR INVITATIONS

In my own experience, I struggled to find my way back into a world that suddenly felt unrecognizable. When Jenna passed, her younger sisters were just 11 and 9. Our family has always been rooted in soccer, and only a week after Jenna's passing, my youngest daughter had an important game. Two days after we buried Jenna, I pushed myself to show up at that game. But truthfully, I wasn't ready. I sat in the car the entire time, watching the game from the passenger seat as if I were at a drive-in movie. It was a small step—more a gesture toward life than an actual return to it—and that was enough for me at that moment.

Declining social invitations or offers of support often makes sense when you're deep in grief, as it can feel like an additional burden to engage with the world when your heart just isn't ready. Taking the time you need to heal is important, but there also comes a point when gently integrating back into life becomes essential. This doesn't mean you're "moving on" or leaving your grief behind—it simply means you're finding ways to live alongside it. At first, even the smallest steps may feel impossible, but honoring your emotional limits while slowly challenging yourself to reconnect can, over time, help rebuild a sense of connection, resilience, and hope.

As you navigate this process, it's equally important to consider how you communicate when declining support or invitations. Expressing appreciation for the offer and encouraging others to keep asking can help maintain those vital connections for when you feel ready to re-engage. When you explain that you're not prepared yet but may be in the future, you create a sense of safety and openness, ensuring others don't interpret your response as rejection. This honors your emotional needs and helps preserve relationships that will be mean-ingful when you're ready to take those steps forward.

Here are 10 respectful ways to decline an invitation or offer, keeping in mind the importance of expressing gratitude and maintaining connection:

1. *"Thank you so much for thinking of me. I'm not ready to join just yet, but your invitation means a lot—please keep me in mind in the future."*
2. *"I really appreciate you reaching out. I'm not in a headspace where I can say yes right now, but it helps to know you're thinking of me."*
3. *"I'd love to take you up on this when I feel a bit more ready. For now, I'm focusing on taking things day by day."*
4. *"Thank you for the invitation. I'm not quite ready to socialize yet, but it means so much to know you're here for me."*
5. *"I'm grateful for your thoughtfulness. I need some more time before I can participate, but your offer doesn't go unnoticed."*
6. *"I appreciate you checking in. Right now, I'm finding it hard to say yes, but I hope you'll continue to ask because I'll let you know when I'm ready."*

7. *"Your kindness means a lot to me. I can't join this time, but I'll keep your offer in mind for the future."*
8. *"It's so thoughtful of you to include me. I'm not quite there yet, but it gives me comfort knowing I have your support."*
9. *"I need to take things slow for now, but please know how much I value your gesture—it really does help me feel supported."*
10. *"Thank you for inviting me. I'm not ready right now, but it means the world to know you're thinking of me."*

By using responses like these, you express both your gratitude and your boundaries. You're giving others a clear message that their offers are appreciated, even if you're not ready to accept them yet, and encouraging them to continue including you when the time feels right. Over time, these small acts of connection can help pave the way toward re-entering life at a pace that feels manageable for you.

NAVIGATING SOCIAL MISSTEPS

One of the hardest parts about re-engaging with the world after loss —if I'm being completely honest—is navigating the social missteps of others. Even the most well-meaning comments can land awkwardly, leaving you feeling misunderstood, frustrated, or even more isolated. It's not that people are trying to be insensitive, they're often just sharing their lives, unaware of how deeply their words might cut. I remember the ache of that all too well. Jenna passed away at the end of her eighth-grade year. The next school year should have been filled with firsts: her first day of high school, home-coming, football games, late-night chats about friends and crushes. All of it was gone—those moments we had imagined, gone in the blink of an eye.

So, when other parents talked about those milestones—their kids' excitement for their first day of high school, the dress shopping for homecoming, the pride in seeing them grow—it felt like a fresh wound every time. The crazy part is they weren't doing anything wrong. They weren't being cruel or thoughtless. They were just living their lives and sharing their joy. But I was so raw, so tender, that even hearing those innocent stories felt unbearable. And you know what? That sensitivity was justified. It wasn't a sign of weakness or overreaction—it was simply the reality of my grief.

What I've come to understand is that these moments don't hurt because people are unkind. They hurt because they're a reminder of what we've lost. And while we can't control the world around us, we can control how we respond to it. Sometimes that means excusing yourself from the conversation. Sometimes it means letting yourself cry in the car afterward. And sometimes, it's as simple as reminding yourself that it's okay to feel tender—it's okay to feel everything.

Grief can make the ordinary feel extraordinary in its weight, and it's not about shutting those feelings down. It's about acknowledging them, letting them pass through, and giving yourself the space you need in that moment to process your emotions. You're not overreacting, you're grieving, and that's the most human thing in the world.

At the same time, grief often brings a layer of complexity to interactions that go beyond people simply sharing their joy or milestones. Sometimes, it's not just someone sharing their life that stings—it's when people try to relate their grief to yours or compare their experiences to what you're going through. Phrases like "I know how you feel" or "When I lost my loved one, I felt the same way" might come from a genuine place of empathy, but they can unintentionally feel dismissive, as though your pain is being minimized, normalized, or folded into their own experience.

These moments can be especially challenging because they can leave you feeling insignificant and alone in your grief, even when someone is trying to connect. That's why holding both compassion and boundaries is essential. You might gently respond to "I know how you feel" with something like, "I appreciate you trying to connect, but this feels very personal to me." Or if someone says, "They're in a better place now," it's okay to reply, "Thank you, but I'm still working through what this loss means to me." These kinds of responses aren't about shutting people down, they're about protecting your emotional space while helping others understand the unique nature of your grief. And these aren't walls you are putting up; they're guardrails that help you navigate the unpredictability of grief in a way that feels safe and manageable for you.

The truth is that these social dynamics require patience—both with yourself and with others. Most people aren't trying to hurt us; they're doing the best they can with the tools they have. By communicating with them and responding with kindness, when possible, you create a safer emotional space for yourself while also giving others the opportunity to learn how to support you in ways that respect your journey.

Grief is complex and navigating social interactions while grieving can feel equally complicated. But when you approach these moments with a mix of grace and self-compassion, you slowly begin to find your footing again. It's not about getting it perfect, it's about honoring your own healing while allowing space for connection on your terms. Whether someone is sharing their life or trying to relate it to yours, it's okay to prioritize your well-being while navigating these interactions with care. It also takes a bit of bravery, but you might be surprised by the strength and courage that lies within you —you can do this.

4
BUILDING RESILIENCE AND EMOTIONAL TOOLS

When I was a little girl, I was never the smartest, fastest, prettiest, or anything "most." I was, in almost every way, average. I didn't stand out in the classroom or on the playground, and I certainly wasn't the star of any team. But if there was one thing I had, it was this quiet, persistent ability to keep trying. I wasn't the best, but I showed up. I kept raising my bar —not to compete with anyone else, but to see how far I could go. Maybe being average is what made me hungry to be better. Perhaps it gave me the freedom to focus on effort rather than perfection. When I wasn't the best, the smartest, or the most talented, I learned to rely on grit and determination. I showed up, worked hard, and found meaning in the process—not just the outcome.

Being average taught me that growth isn't reserved for the naturally gifted. It's available to anyone willing to put in the effort, to keep going when it's hard, and to believe in the possibility of becoming more. I wasn't weighed down by the pressure to be perfect; instead, I was driven by the curiosity to see how far I could go.

Looking back, I realize that the greatest lessons of my life didn't come from standing at the top; they came from the climb. And being average wasn't a limitation—it was a gift. A gift that taught me how to work hard, stay humble, and trust in my ability to grow.

I look back now and see how my parents played a role in shaping that part of me. They were tough, hardworking, and practical people who didn't hand out praise for every little thing, but they didn't let me give up, either. When things got hard, their response was simple: "Keep going." So, I did. I learned I didn't need to be the best; I just needed to keep pressing forward.

That lesson stayed with me and profoundly influenced my view of resilience. Resilience isn't about being the strongest or the fastest or getting it right every time. It's about showing up—especially when life knocks you down. It's about pressing forward when the road feels impossibly hard and trusting that the effort will lead you somewhere meaningful, even if you can't see it yet.

As I've walked through grief, that self-imposed expectation that "I can do this" has taken on a deeper meaning. It's not about pretending I have it all figured out or shouldering the weight of loss alone. It's about acknowledging that resilience doesn't mean bypassing pain; it means allowing myself to feel it, face it, and keep moving through it.

I've learned resilience is the courage to keep trying, even when your heart feels shattered, and you wonder what's the use. It's the ability to bend without breaking, to find small moments of hope amid despair. Building resilience isn't about ignoring grief; it's about integrating it into the fabric of who you are—like climbing the steps of a ladder. Each step and experience becomes part of your foundation, lifting you higher with every effort. The grief doesn't disappear; it becomes a steady rung beneath your feet, supporting your growth as you move toward healing.

This chapter explores how resilience, mindfulness, and therapeutic writing can become powerful tools in navigating the heartache of losing someone you love. These practices don't erase what you're going through. Still, they give you a way to keep showing up for yourself—to keep pressing forward, one step at a time, with the same quiet persistence that once helped a little girl believe she could keep raising her bar.

BUILDING RESILIENCE THROUGH SMALL, DAILY ACTS

Resilience doesn't always look fancy or noticeable to the outside world. Sometimes, it's just the quiet, steady effort to keep going, even when no one sees it. And it is often nurtured in the small, seemingly mundane acts of daily life. These small steps help create a sense of structure and stability, anchoring you as you navigate the chaos of grief. Admiral William H. McRaven, author of *Make Your Bed: Little Things That Can Change Your Life... And Maybe the World* writes about the power of starting your day with simple tasks like making your bed. This small act sets the tone for the day, offering a sense of accomplishment and control, no matter how turbulent the rest of your life may feel.

In grief, these small daily acts can foster resilience in profound ways. Waking up and making your bed might seem trivial, but it's a tangible reminder that you've taken a step forward, however small. Putting on clean clothes you can go out in, even when it feels like a monumental effort, is a quiet act of self-care. Sitting outside in the fresh air or taking a short walk allows you to reconnect with the world around you, even if you're not yet ready to re-engage fully.

Writing down just one thought or feeling each day can help create clarity and release. Similarly, practicing mindfulness—whether through a few minutes of deep breathing, focusing on the sensations of your body, or noticing the sounds and sights around you—can help ground you in the present moment. As Eckhart Tolle, author of

The Power of Now, says, "Rather than being your thoughts and emotions, be the awareness behind them." This perspective reminds us that by observing our emotions without judgment, we allow them to flow through us rather than becoming trapped in them. Becoming a witness to our thoughts and feelings creates a powerful shift—from reactive to reflective. We gain clarity and control when we step back and observe, realizing that emotions are temporary visitors, not permanent truths. These small, intentional actions, like mindful observation and journaling, create space for healing and empower us to respond with greater wisdom and compassion.

These acts may feel insignificant on their own. Still, together, they are a powerful way of showing up for yourself—like putting on your oxygen mask before assisting others. These small habits remind you that tending to your emotional and physical well-being is not selfish but essential. Just as you can't pour from an empty cup, you can't navigate the complexities of grief without first nurturing yourself. Over time, these small, intentional practices create a ripple effect, gradually building your resilience and helping you feel more capable, connected, and present. As you begin to care for yourself, these acts also become a beacon—a guiding light for your family and loved ones, showing them that healing is possible, and that hope can take root and grow even in the darkest moments.

Resilience doesn't mean leaping over the chasm of grief in a single bound. It means slowly, gently finding your footing, one step at a time. By focusing on small, daily actions, you remind yourself that you can create moments of stability and care even amid pain. And in those moments, you are planting the seeds of healing.

REFLECTION EXERCISE: A RECIPE FOR RESILIENCE

This exercise invites you to step outside your grief momentarily and reflect on a time in your life when you demonstrated resilience. Think of a challenge you overcame, no matter how big or small. The goal is to remind yourself that resilience isn't something you're building from scratch, it's already within you. If you've done it before, even in the smallest of ways, you can draw on those same strengths and retake steps toward resilience. Think of this as uncovering your personal "recipe" for resilience—what ingredients helped you overcome difficulty and how you might use them again.

Use these guiding questions to explore your past experiences with resilience:

- **Can you recall when you faced a significant challenge or difficulty in your life? What was the situation?**
- **What inner strengths did you lean on to help you navigate that challenge? (For example: patience, determination, adaptability, creativity.)**
- **What steps did you take, even small ones, that helped you begin to move forward?**
- **Did you rely on external support, such as friends, family, a therapist, or mentors? If so, how did they support you?**
- **How did you cope with the emotional toll of that experience? Did you journal, talk to someone, or find comfort in daily habits?**
- **What lessons did you take from that experience about your ability to endure and persevere?**
- **What emotions did you feel when you overcame that challenge? Can you draw on those feelings again as a source of strength?**
- **What strategies from that experience might you apply to your current journey through grief?**
- **What would you say to them if you were advising someone facing a similar challenge? Can you offer that same advice to yourself now?**

The idea is not to minimize your grief but to gently remind yourself of the resilience you already possess. These reflections can act as a bridge, connecting the strength you've demonstrated in the past to the steps you're taking today. Resilience isn't about perfection, it's about trying, adjusting, and finding ways to move forward, even when the path feels uncertain.

Just like a recipe combines many ingredients to create something whole, you build resilience through small, intentional acts. By revisiting a time when you practiced resilience, you're rediscovering the ingredients that work for you, helping you craft a way forward through this moment of loss. You've done it before—and you can do it again.

CREATING A RESILIENCE TOOLKIT

When I was a little girl, I asked my dad what his favorite tree was. Without missing a beat, he said, "A willow tree." Naturally curious, I asked him why—why not a sturdy oak or a towering pine? All these years later, his answer has stayed with me.

He told me that willow trees are remarkable because of their flexibility. Their branches, though appearing delicate, are incredibly resilient—designed to bend with the wind without breaking. He explained that a willow's roots spread wide, giving them stability and the movement needed to survive and thrive, even in the fiercest storms. Willows are adapted to grow in areas prone to floods, hurricanes, and high winds, thriving in conditions that might topple other trees.

That conversation was a teachable moment, one of those seemingly ordinary exchanges that transform into something profound. My dad shared that he'd always tried to live like a willow tree. He wanted to be strong enough to weather life's storms, flexible enough to bend without breaking, and grounded by a foundation broad enough to hold him and his family up. This message, coming from a man who endured so much trauma in his life, has always been profoundly powerful to me.

Reflecting on his words now, especially in the context of grief, I see how much wisdom there is in the willow's example. Resilience isn't about being unyielding or impervious to pain—it's about having the strength to endure and the flexibility to adapt. It's about spreading your roots, finding those sources of support and stability that keep you grounded—and allowing yourself the grace to bend, sway, and move by the winds of life without snapping.

In our most challenging moments, those that threaten to uproot us entirely, resilience is the gentle but unbreakable reminder that we can bend and still stand. Like the willow, the storm tests us, but our roots hold us firmly in place. And when the winds pass, we find we're still here—perhaps changed, perhaps a bit weathered, but undeniably alive and still reaching for the sky.

Building resilience is an active process that involves leaning on old helpful habits, learning new behaviors, and developing a mindset that supports healing. The American Psychological Association notes that resilience can be cultivated through thoughts, actions, and behaviors that promote growth. One practical tool is gratitude journaling. By regularly writing down things you're thankful for, even small ones, you shift your focus toward the positive aspects of life. This practice offers a counterbalance, fostering hope and a sense of equilibrium in the face of grief. Gratitude journaling has been shown to enhance emotional well-being, providing a little light on days that feel particularly dark. It's a gentle reminder that beauty and kindness still exist even amidst loss.

Another tool for resilience is establishing daily rituals that promote emotional grounding. These routines offer stability and a sense of control during times when life feels anything but predictable. Simple rituals—such as morning meditation, evening reflections, or lighting a candle—can anchor your emotions and reduce anxiety. After losing my father, I began writing to him and reflecting on all the reasons I cherish him. This simple yet profound practice brought comfort and a continued sense of connection. It became a moment of peace in my day, a ritual that reminded me of the enduring bond we will always share.

To cultivate resilience, consider creating a personal resilience toolbox. This toolbox is a collection of practices, habits, and resources that support your emotional well-being and help you navigate challenging times. Below are some ideas to consider including in your toolbox:

- **Gratitude journaling**: Write down three things you're grateful for each day.
- **Daily rituals**: Establish grounding habits, such as making your bed first thing in the morning, lighting a candle, or setting intentions for the day.
- **Mindfulness or meditation**: Spend a few minutes focusing on your breath or observing your thoughts without judgment.
- **Physical movement**: Incorporate walking, yoga, or another form of exercise to release tension and improve your mood.
- **Connecting with nature**: Spend time outdoors to find peace and perspective in the natural world.
- **Creative expression**: Engage in art, music, dance, or writing to express your emotions.
- **Deep breathing exercises**: Practice box breathing to reduce stress and anxiety.
- **Journaling**: Reflect on your feelings, experiences, or memories in a safe, private space.
- **Therapy or counseling**: Seek professional guidance to process your emotions and gain new insights.

- **Support groups**: Join a community of others who understand and share your experiences.
- **Acts of kindness**: Volunteer or help others to create a sense of purpose and connection.
- **Reading inspirational material**: Explore books, essays, or quotes that resonate with you.
- **Spiritual or religious practices**: Lean into prayer, meditation, or other faith-based activities if they bring comfort.
- **Self-compassion practices**: Speak to yourself with kindness, as you would to a close friend.
- **Healthy sleep habits**: Prioritize rest and create a bedtime routine that promotes relaxation.
- **Balanced nutrition**: Fuel your body with foods nourishing and supporting your physical health.
- **Celebrating small wins**: Acknowledge and appreciate even the tiniest steps forward.
- **Reaching out for support**: Ask for help from friends, family, or mentors when needed.
- **Visualization**: Imagine a safe, calming space or visualize yourself overcoming a challenge.

In the quiet moments of reflection, you might discover inner strengths you hadn't recognized before. These strengths become your allies in grief, enabling you to navigate the turbulent waters more easily. You may find solace in nature, where the steady rhythm of the world continues its course, offering reminders of life's cycles and the lessons nature can teach us. It could be through creativity, where you can express your emotions without words, painting, or shaping them into something tangible. These strengths, these roots, are what sustain you when the winds of grief blow hard. They ground you in the present, allowing you to face each day with more courage and hope.

As you explore these tools and incorporate them into your daily life, remember that resilience is not a destination but a process. It's about finding what works for you, what helps you feel grounded and connected to both your loved one and yourself. Building a resilience toolkit is an ongoing journey of self-discovery and acceptance, where you learn to live with love and loss intertwined. It's about nurturing the parts of you that remain strong even when you feel most vulnerable and allowing those parts to guide you toward moments of joy and connection. Through resilience, you find the strength to carry your grief and love forward, honoring the past while embracing the future.

MINDFULNESS PRACTICES FOR GRIEF: BUILDING TOOLS FOR CHALLENGING EMOTIONS

When practiced thoughtfully, mindfulness can offer solace during grief by grounding you in the present moment. However, renowned trauma expert Dr. Bessel van der Kolk explains in *The Body Keeps the Score* that mindfulness must be approached carefully, especially when emotions and physical sensations are overwhelming. Diving into mindfulness practices too quickly or without the proper tools can risk reactivating painful memories or emotional responses. Instead, building a foundation of safety and stability before engaging deeply with mindfulness practices is essential. Dr. van der Kolk emphasizes that mindfulness should begin slowly, giving you the space to feel your emotions in manageable increments while providing tools to regulate overwhelming sensations. Below, I've outlined practical advice and gentle steps for cultivating mindfulness in a way that fosters healing without becoming overwhelming for you.

START SMALL: BUILDING A FOUNDATION OF SAFETY

Before diving into intensive mindfulness practices, it's important to establish a sense of safety within your body and mind. Here are some foundational practices to ease into mindfulness:

1. **Grounding Exercises**: Begin with simple grounding techniques, like placing your feet firmly on the floor and noticing the sensation of contact. This reminds your body and mind that you are here, in the present moment, and safe.
2. **Anchor with the Breath**: Focus on basic breathing exercises, such as counting your breaths or gently extending your exhalation. For example, try inhaling for three seconds, holding for three, and exhaling for six. This creates a calming rhythm without overwhelming your nervous system.
3. **Short Sessions**: Start with mindfulness practices that last just 1-2 minutes. Over time, as you feel more comfortable, you can gradually increase the duration.

GENTLE PRACTICES TO EXPLORE MINDFULNESS

As you feel ready, you can begin to expand your mindfulness practice with these tools:

1. **Deep Breathing**

- The **4-7-8 Method**: Inhale for four seconds, hold for seven seconds and exhale for eight seconds. This technique activates the parasympathetic nervous system, helping to regulate emotional intensity.
- Please focus on the sensation of air entering and leaving your body, noticing how it feels as your chest rises and falls.

2. Body Scans

- Lie or sit comfortably and bring awareness to each body part, starting at the top of your head and moving to your toes. If you notice tension, acknowledge it without judgment and breathe into that area.
- Dr. van der Kolk notes that body scans help reconnect you to your physical self and reveal where grief might manifest as tension or discomfort.

3. Sensory Awareness

- Use your senses to anchor yourself in the present moment. Look around and identify:
  - Five things you can see
  - Four things you can feel
  - Three things you can hear
  - Two things you can smell
  - One thing you can taste
- This "5-4-3-2-1" technique brings your attention to your immediate surroundings and away from overwhelming thoughts and traumas from your past.

4. Mindful Walking

- Walk slowly, paying attention to the sensation of your feet touching the ground. Notice the rhythm of your steps and your breath. Let the act of walking become meditation, grounding you in the here and now.

5. Journaling for Emotional Safety

- Start with simple prompts, such as:
  - "What am I feeling right now?"

- ○ "What sensations do I notice in my body?"
  - ○ "What is one small thing I can do to feel more grounded today?"
- Journaling allows you to observe and release your emotions in a structured and safe way.

TOOLS TO NAVIGATE DIFFICULT EMOTIONS

When mindfulness brings up challenging emotions or physical sensations, it's crucial to have tools to navigate them effectively:

1. **Self-Soothing Techniques**:
   - ○ Hold a comforting object, like a soft blanket or a small stone, to remind yourself of safety.
   - ○ Wrap yourself in a blanket or place a hand on your chest to contain yourself.
2. **Distraction Strategies**:
   - ○ Engage in a simple, grounding activity, such as folding laundry, doodling, or sipping a warm drink. These actions can help shift your focus when emotions feel overwhelming.
3. **Setting Boundaries with Mindfulness**:
   - ○ If a practice feels too intense, allow yourself to step back. For example, focus only on your hands or feet instead of a full body scan.
4. **Connecting with Nature**:
   - ○ Sit outside and observe the natural world, the rustling of leaves, the warmth of the sun, or the coolness of a breeze. Nature's steady rhythm can help you regulate your emotions.
5. **Seek Professional Guidance**:
   - ○ Suppose mindfulness practices consistently bring up distressing emotions or memories. In that case, it's worth noting that grief can sometimes become

complicated and may require additional support. In these moments, working with a trauma-informed therapist can provide a safe and compassionate space to process both your emotions and the unique weight of your loss.

Mindfulness is about gently cultivating awareness, moment by moment, and creating a sense of stability within yourself. Over time, these small practices become tools in your resilience toolkit, helping you face grief with compassion and strength.

Louise Hay writes, "I am willing to release the need to be unkind to myself as I process this pain. I allow myself to feel, heal, and find peace in my own time." This perspective invites you to approach mindfulness as a process of self-discovery and gentle growth. With patience and self-compassion, mindfulness allows you to observe your grief with curiosity and kindness, creating a safe space to heal while honoring the love and loss you carry.

WRITING AS A HEALING PRACTICE

When I reflect on the power of writing, I am reminded of the lessons I learned from my grief counselor, Kathryn and the solace I found through journaling after Jenna's passing. Journaling became more than just a practice for me—it became a lifeline. I had always been aware of the therapeutic benefits of putting pen to paper. Still, it wasn't until Kathryn introduced me to journaling as a way to process emotions and connect on a deeper level that it became a transformative tool. It's a practice I continue to this day, years later, because of its clarity and connection.

I'll never forget when Kathryn first explained the power of journaling. She described it as a safe space where thoughts, emotions, and even unspoken questions could live without judgment. Her advice was simple yet profound: Let the words flow freely, even if they don't initially make sense. Trust that the act of writing would eventually bring clarity and in that clarity, healing.

Although I had written to my dad after he passed, the guidance Kathryn provided enriched my journaling experience in ways I hadn't anticipated. This practice became more than just a release—it became a bridge, a way to connect with Jenna and gently explore the intricate layers of my grief. With Kathryn's encouragement, I approached journaling with intention, often beginning with a single, grounding question like, "What do I need to feel today?" or "How can I honor you, Jenna?"

Over time, these entries evolved into a heartfelt dialogue conversation between my grief and resilience. I'll never forget the day I wrote to Jenna, asking for a sign in the clouds. Later that day, as I looked to the sky, I saw a rainbow unlike any I'd seen. It didn't arch across the horizon like a traditional rainbow; instead, it smiled high in the sky, its colors vibrant and luminous. I felt an undeniable connection in that moment, as though Jenna had answered me with love and reassurance. It was a deeply moving reminder of how journaling could invite not just healing but moments of profound connection and hope.

JOURNALING AS A TOOL FOR RESILIENCE

Writing is not just a way to process grief; it's a way to foster resilience. By committing to small, consistent acts of reflection, you can begin to build a journaling practice that supports your emotional well-being and helps you navigate the complexities of loss.

Here are some practical tips to help you with your journaling journey:

- **Start Small**: If journaling feels overwhelming, begin with a single sentence or thought each day. For example, "Today I feel.... because ."

- **Create a Dedicated Space**: Find a quiet, comfortable place where you feel safe to write. This could be a cozy corner in your home or even a peaceful spot in nature. Initially, I would journal at the cemetery and sit among the trees. It made me feel deeply connected to Jenna.
- **Use Prompts to Get Started**: Try using guided questions to ease into writing, such as:
  - What is one memory with my loved one that brings me comfort?
  - What emotions am I feeling right now, and where do I feel them in my body?
  - What would it be if I could say anything to my loved one today?
  - What small step can I take today to care for myself?
- **Write Letters**: Write a letter to your loved one, expressing what you're feeling or wish to share with them.
- **Focus on Gratitude**: Dedicate a portion of your journaling to writing down three things you're grateful for each day, even if they're small. Gratitude can help shift your perspective over time.
- **Don't Edit Yourself**: Let your thoughts flow freely without worrying about grammar, structure, or "getting it right." This is your space to be raw and honest.
- **Explore Your Inner Landscape**: Write about what resilience means to you and reflect on a time when you overcame a challenge. What strengths did you draw upon, and how might those strengths help you now?
- **Write About Your Goals:** Reflect on your big or small goals and share them with your loved one through your writing. Invite them into your journey by imagining the advice or encouragement they might offer. Write about why achieving these goals feels necessary, especially if they

connect to honoring their memory. This practice can help you stay motivated and feel supported, even in their absence.

- **Acknowledge Signs**: Write about any signs or symbols that remind you of your loved one. Reflect on how these moments make you feel and what they mean.
- **Incorporate Spirituality**: If it resonates with you, include a prayer, mantra, or intention at the start or end of your journaling session.

A PRACTICE THAT EVOLVES

Over time, your journaling practice may evolve, just as mine did. What begins as a tool to release heavy emotions can grow into a way to reconnect with hope and joy. Journaling allows you to honor the depth of your grief while making space for healing and renewal. It also continues your relationship with your loved one, giving you a space to express your love, share your thoughts, and feel their presence in a new, meaningful way.

When you commit to showing up for yourself on the page, even for a few minutes a day, you're taking an active step toward resilience. This practice isn't about perfection or productivity, it's about presence. Each word you write reminds you that your grief, love, and healing all matter. As you continue this journey, your journal will become more than a tool; it will be a companion, guiding you through the waves of loss and into the light of new beginnings.

In the next chapter, we'll explore how to carry the love you've shared forward, finding ways to honor the life of your loved one while embracing the path ahead.

MAKE A DIFFERENCE WITH YOUR REVIEW

Sharing Your Story Helps Someone Else Find Theirs

"Grief shared is grief lessened." – Unknown

Grief can feel like a lonely road, but the truth is, none of us walk it alone. Somewhere out there, someone is looking for words that will help them make sense of their own loss. Someone needs to know they're not the only one feeling this way.

Your review could be the reason they pick up this book. It could be the reason they find comfort in knowing their grief isn't something to fix—it's something to carry with love.

★ ★ ★ ★ ★

Why Your Review Matters

Most people choose books based on what others say. When you share your thoughts, you help another grieving heart find a place where they feel seen, understood, and supported. Your review could help...

- ...one more grieving soul feel less alone.
- ...one more person realize they don't have to "move on" to heal.
- ...one more heart find hope in the midst of loss.
- ...one more loved one be remembered in a way that feels right.

How to Leave a Review

It's simple, free, and only takes a minute. Just scan the QR code below or visit:

If this book has meant something to you, your words might mean everything to someone else.

With all my love—thank you.

Dena M. Derenale Betti

5
HONORING AND CARRYING
LOVE FORWARD

After Jenna passed away, an outpouring of generosity surrounded our family in a way I could never have imagined. Her third-grade teacher started a memorial fund on our behalf, and donations flooded in from friends, family, and people we had never met. The kindness was overwhelming. We used much of the money to pay for Jenna's burial services, but there was still money left after all the expenses.

I immediately knew I wanted to return that remaining generosity to the world in Jenna's honor. That desire gave birth to #hersmile, a nonprofit dedicated to supporting families like ours—families who have experienced the devastating loss of a dependent child or the loss of a parent with dependent children.

Through #hersmile, I discovered something profound about myself: I grieve by doing. I needed to put action behind my grief; to take all the love I carried for Jenna and find a way to express it in the world. The nonprofit became more than just a way to help others—it became a lifeline in my healing. It allowed me to channel my sorrow into something meaningful, transforming the weight of my grief into a force for good.

Grief has no roadmap, but for me, creating #hersmile was a way to navigate the uncharted territory of loss. It allowed me to live my love for Jenna outwardly—to weave her spirit into the fabric of everyday life. I found solace in the idea that while I could no longer mother Jenna in a traditional sense, I could still honor her by lifting others who faced the unimaginable.

Over time, I realized that honoring her wasn't just about remembering the past but about carrying her forward with me. Whenever #hersmile supported a grieving family, I felt Jenna's presence. Every act of kindness in her name was a reminder that love never dies; it simply changes form.

Grief is often painted as something to endure, but I've seen it as something to engage with—to shape, mold, and transform. My journey with #hersmile has shown me that healing doesn't mean leaving our loved ones behind; it means finding ways to keep them woven into the story of our lives and making sure the world is better because of them.

In this chapter, I invite you to consider what brings you comfort. Whether through small rituals, creative expressions, or acts of service, honoring your loved one's memory can guide your healing. Grief, after all, is love with nowhere to go—until we choose to send it back into the world.

WAYS TO HONOR YOUR LOVED ONE'S MEMORY

Honoring a loved one can take many forms, from grand tributes to small, everyday rituals. The most meaningful acts resonate deeply with you, allowing your loved one's presence to continue in your life in a way that feels personal and healing. Our family started the **Jenna Betti Memorial Golf Tournament** to channel our grief into something positive and meaningful. It was born from a desire to gather the community, celebrate Jenna's life, and turn heartbreak into action. Each year, it becomes an incredible day filled with love, laughter, and friendship, coupled with the immense generosity we pay into the world in Jenna's honor. The tournament not only keeps her spirit alive but also supports families who have experienced profound loss, helping them navigate their journeys through grief. It's a reminder that even in sorrow, there can be joy, connection, and a lasting impact.

Here are a variety of ways—both big and small—that you can consider:

1. Organizing Events in Their Honor

- **Host a Memorial Golf Tournament or Charity Event -** Like the **Jenna Betti Memorial Golf Tournament**, events bring people together in celebration and remembrance, creating a ripple of generosity.
- **Create an Annual Walk or Run** – Many honor loved ones by organizing a community walk, 5K run, or bike ride that raises funds for a cause they cared about.
- **Host a Scholarship Program** – Establish a scholarship in their name to help students pursue education in a field that mattered to them.

2. Acts of Kindness and Giving

- **Perform Random Acts of Kindness** – Do small, unexpected acts of kindness in their memory (e.g., paying for someone's coffee, leaving kind notes for strangers, donating to shelters).
- **Start a Pay-It-Forward Initiative** – Give away a certain number of gifts, meals, or donations in their name and encourage others to do the same.

- **Adopt a Family in Need** – Support a family during the holidays or difficult times to honor your loved one.

3. Personal Rituals and Reflection Practices

- **Light a Candle** – A simple yet profound way to create a moment of connection.
- **Write Letters to Them** – Journaling or writing letters as if speaking to them can be profoundly healing.
- **Visit a Special Place** – Whether it's their favorite park, a beach, or a quiet spot, revisiting places they loved can bring comfort.
- **Set Up a Memory Table or Altar** – Create a space in your home with their photos, a favorite object, or a candle.
- **Speak Their Name Often** – Simply sharing their name in conversation keeps their memory alive.

4. Legacy and Creativity

- **Write a Book or Blog About Their Story** – Share their life, your memories, or their impact on others.
- **Plant a Tree or Garden in Their Honor** – Watching something grow in their name is a beautiful reminder of their lasting impact.
- **Create a Playlist of Their Favorite Songs** – Listen when you need to feel close to them.
- **Make a Memory Quilt or Scrapbook** – Gather old photos, notes, and mementos to weave a tangible reminder of their life together.
- **Create Art or Poetry Inspired by Them** – Expressing emotions through creativity can be cathartic.

5. Giving Back and Community Support

- **Start a Nonprofit or Foundation** – If they had a cause they were passionate about, a nonprofit can continue their mission.
- **Volunteer in Their Name** – Dedicate time to organizations they supported, such as shelters, youth programs, or environmental causes.
- **Sponsor a Bench, Park, or Playground** – Many communities allow for dedications in loved ones' names.
- **Donate in Their Name** – Whether to a hospital, library, school, or charity, donations can make a meaningful difference.

6. Celebrating Special Days

- **Honor Their Birthday With a Special Tradition** – Gather with family and friends to celebrate their life.
- **Acknowledge Their Angelversary** – Mark the anniversary of their passing with a meaningful ritual or act of kindness.
- **Create a 'Memory Jar'** – Family and friends can contribute memories and read them together on special days.

7. Living Out Their Legacy

- **Embrace Their Passions** – If they loved cooking, sports, or hiking, continue those activities in their honor.
- **Carry Forward Their Values** – If they were known for generosity, humor, or resilience, embody those traits daily.
- **Share Their Wisdom** – Pass down their favorite quotes, life lessons, and traditions to the next generation.

How you honor your loved one is deeply personal—there's no right or wrong way to do it, only what feels true to your heart. For us, it has meant starting the #hersmile Nonprofit, hosting an annual golf tournament, establishing a local high school scholarship that celebrates the values Jenna embodied, and even planting trees in her honor. Each of these acts is a thread in the fabric of our love for her, a way to ensure that her light continues to touch the world.

Grief doesn't have to be something we endure—it can be something we engage with, shape, and transform. Every time we honor Jenna in these ways, we live our love out loud. And what a powerful way to love—to turn loss into something that creates connection, impact, and meaning. Because love doesn't disappear; it just asks us to find new ways to express it.

THE UNSEEN ECHOES OF LOVE

There was a time when they believed they had done everything right. Their daughter, Lena, was quiet but not withdrawn, sensitive but not fragile. She had always been the one who left little notes on the counter, scribbled in the margins of old notebooks, messages that once felt like whispers of her soul: *Love you, Mom. Love you, Dad.* And then, one day, she was gone.

It happened on an afternoon like any other. The house still carried the warmth of breakfast; the dishes from lunch sat waiting in the sink. There was no warning, no moment to brace themselves—just silence—and then a before and an after.

For weeks, Claire and David moved like ghosts inside their own home. The walls were too still, her absence too loud. They searched the past like archaeologists, looking for the thing they had missed— the sign, the moment, the plea hidden beneath her quietness. But all they found were memories, unalterable and merciless. The guilt became an unrelenting tide, pulling them under again and again.

It wasn't until a stranger—a mother from a support group—placed her hand over Claire's and said, *"Your love didn't fail her. Your love is still here, waiting for you to give it a place to go.",* that something shifted.

That night, Claire and David sat at the kitchen table where Lena once did her homework, where she had rested her chin in her hands, dreaming of futures they would never get to see. And they made a decision.

If they could not go back and change the past, they would move forward and change the future.

TURNING PAIN INTO PURPOSE

It started as a simple conversation. A quiet hope whispered between them—that no other parent should wake up to the hollow ache of loss, that no other teenager should feel so alone. They would take Lena's story and carry it where it needed to be heard. They would speak to the ones who might be standing in the same darkness she had—before it was too late.

Claire's hands trembled the first time they spoke at a high school. David's voice caught in his throat. But when they looked into the eyes of the students—some skeptical, some afraid, some silently nodding as if they understood—something inside them settled.

They spoke about Lena's laughter, her dreams, and her struggles. They talked about how easily someone can hide pain behind a smile and how even the most loving parents can miss the quiet signs of suffering. And most importantly, they spoke about hope.

"If you're hurting, if you feel like there's no way forward, I promise you— there is," Claire would say, her voice steady now. *"Talk to someone. Let someone in. The world needs you, even when you can't see it. And if you think no one cares, know that we do."*

David would step forward then, his voice lower but resolute. *"And for those of you who see someone struggling—say something. Be the person who reaches out. It could be the difference between life and loss."*

THE ECHOES OF LOVE LIVE ON

The talks grew. More schools, more conversations. More letters from students who had found the courage to ask for help, from parents who had learned to listen more closely.

But it wasn't just the students who were changed. Claire and David began to breathe again.

Their grief did not disappear. It never would. But it found motion, found purpose. They discovered that love does not die when the person dies. It lingers, waiting to be shaped into something new.

And so, they continued.

They spoke for Lena.

They spoke for the ones still here, searching for hope.

They spoke for love—the kind that does not end, the type that keeps reaching forward, again and again.

A LEGACY OF LOVE: CHOOSING HOPE OVER ANGER

Grief is deeply personal, and no two people experience it the same way. Lena's parents found their way through their sorrow by turning outward, sharing their daughter's story, and using their pain to help others. Their grief became a bridge—an offering of love and hope to those who most needed it.

But grief doesn't always unfold that way. Some carry their loss differently, quietly, letting it shape their world in ways they don't fully understand. Instead of reaching outward, they turn inward, holding onto their pain so tightly that it begins to define them. And when grief is left unattended—when love is buried beneath layers of anger and regret, it doesn't just affect the person carrying it. It seeps into their relationships, choices, and ability to see the world beyond their loss.

Michael's story is one of a man who struggled to move forward. His love for his wife, Rachel, never faded, but over time, it became eclipsed by the pain of losing her. And as the years passed, that grief, unresolved and unspoken, began to cast shadows over the very people who needed him most. Step into his world for a moment. See through his eyes. And ask yourself—how do we honor those we have lost? Is it through holding on to the pain? Or is it through finding a small way to let love lead us forward?

Michael was never the same after his wife, Rachel, passed away. She had beaten cancer once before they had even met, and he had believed—naively, perhaps—that it would never come back. But it had. And this time, it took her.

In the early days, he was too consumed by grief to think about anything else. He had a five-year-old daughter, Lily, who needed him, but he was barely functioning. The world had lost its color. Food had no taste. Laughter was foreign. He went through the motions of parenting—packing lunches, reading bedtime stories—but his heart wasn't in it. The life he had built with Rachel had been stolen from him, and in its place, there was only an emptiness he didn't know how to fill.

But grief is a patient thing. It doesn't demand attention—it just lingers like a shadow that refuses to lift. And for Michael, that shadow became something else: anger.

Anger at the doctors for not saving her. Anger at Rachel for not telling him how serious it was. Anger at himself for not realizing it sooner. The rational part of him knew she hadn't hidden anything from him. She had fought as hard as she could right in front of him. But the irrational part—the part ruled by pain—felt *duped*.

The years passed. He raised Lily the best he could, though he often felt he was failing her. He taught her to ride a bike, helped her with homework, and watched her grow into a kind, compassionate young woman. He knew she had Rachel's heart—always looking for the good in people. She was his greatest source of pride.

And then, one day, she met someone.

Ethan was a good man, and Michael knew it. He saw how Ethan looked at Lily, how he adored her, and how he respected her. He should have been happy for his daughter. He should have been grateful that she had found love and wouldn't have to go through life alone.

But he wasn't happy. He was furious.

Not at Ethan. But at life.

Lily had been the one constant in his life, the one thing that tethered him to this world. And now, she was leaving. She was choosing someone else over him. Just like Rachel had—except Rachel hadn't decided to leave, had she?

It didn't matter. The pain felt the same.

At the engagement dinner, he could barely look at her. She was glowing and filled with joy; all he could feel was loss. His love for Rachel sat in the shadow of his anger, buried under years of resentment for how his life had turned out.

It wasn't until weeks later, when Lily finally confronted him, that he realized the truth.

"Dad," she said gently, her voice thick with unshed tears. "Mom would hate this."

And suddenly, it hit him.

Rachel—his Rachel—had spent her life choosing love over anger. Even when she was sick, even when she was in pain, she had never allowed resentment to take root in her heart. She had loved him fiercely, and she had loved their daughter beyond measure. She would have *wanted* this for Lily. She would have wanted *him* to be happy for her.

But he had been stuck in his grief for so long that he hadn't allowed himself to see it.

That night, for the first time in twenty-five years, he sat in front of Rachel's picture and spoke to her. *"I'm sorry,"* he whispered. *"I let you down. I let myself down. And I let Lily down."*

As the words left his lips, something inside him cracked open. Not all at once, but just enough to let the light back in.

He would never stop grieving Rachel. He knew that now. But he also knew that grief wasn't meant to keep him stuck. It was meant to be a bridge—not a wall.

The following day, he picked up the phone and called Lily.

"I want to help you plan the wedding," he said, his voice rough. *"I want to be happy for you because I am. I just forgot how to show it."*

And in that moment, he knew—choosing love would always be the right choice.

HONORING OUR LOVED ONES BY HONORING OURSELVES

Losing someone you love shifts the foundation of your world. It can be tempting—so tempting—to let pain turn into anger, to let love sit behind the shadow of loss. But the truth is, we honor our loved ones best when we refuse to let grief harden us...when we refuse to let it destroy us.

Michael's story is not just about a man who lost his wife—it's about all of us who have known loss and wrestled with the emotions that follow. Pain. Anger. Guilt. Disappointment. They are easy places to go, but *letting them take root in our souls is not okay.*

Love is the legacy we carry forward.

We don't need to make grand gestures. We don't need to start charities or host events—though we can if it calls to us. Sometimes, the most profound way to honor someone is simply by living with an open heart. By allowing joy back in. By seeing the beauty in the world, even when they are no longer here to see it with us.

Love is not meant to be locked away in sorrow.

It is meant to be *lived.*

LIVING WITH LOVE AND LOSS

Navigating the space between love and loss is a delicate dance that requires grace and patience. The absence of a loved one can leave an indelible mark, a void that feels insurmountable. Yet, within this emptiness remains an enduring connection, a love that persists beyond the boundaries of time and space. Balancing this love with the reality of their absence is a nuanced aspect of grieving. It involves acknowledging that moving forward doesn't equate to forgetting. Instead, it's about weaving their memory into the fabric of your ongoing life, allowing their presence to guide you as you grow and evolve.

The dual process model of coping with bereavement suggests that grieving involves a dynamic interplay between confronting the loss and engaging in restorative activities. This oscillation allows you to honor your loved one while continuing to live fully. Some days, you may find yourself enveloped in memories, revisiting the moments you shared, the laughter, and the love. On others, you might engage in activities that bring joy and fulfillment, reminding you of the resilience of the human spirit. This balance is not about erasing the pain but about integrating it into your life in a way that honors both the past and the present.

As you embark on this path, reassuring yourself as you move forward is crucial. Embracing new experiences and finding moments of joy again doesn't diminish the bond you share with your loved one. Instead, it's a testament to their lasting impact on your life, a reflection of the love that continues to bloom in their absence. As Megan Devine eloquently said, *"It's okay not to be okay."* This sentiment highlights the importance of self-compassion in the grieving process. It's about granting yourself the grace to feel the full spectrum of emotions without judgment or expectation. In doing so, you create a space where healing can occur, and love and loss coexist harmoniously.

Yet, the way we navigate grief is deeply personal. For some, healing emerges through action—finding meaning in your loss and sharing your loved one's story. Grief becomes an anchor for others, holding them in place and making it difficult to see beyond the pain. Lena's parents and Michael both carried immense love for the ones they lost, yet their paths through grief could not have been more different. Though shattered by their daughter's passing, Lena's parents found healing in sharing her story. They reached outward, allowing their love for her to become a light that illuminated the way for others. Through their pain, they discovered purpose, and in doing so, they honored the gift of her life.

Michael, however, carried his grief differently. His love for Rachel became buried beneath anger and regret, twisting into resentment over time. He held on so tightly to his loss that he unknowingly closed himself off from the very thing he needed most—connection.

His grief was not a bridge but a wall, keeping him trapped in the past and unable to embrace the love that still existed in his life.

Both stories reveal a truth we often struggle to face: *"Grief is just love with nowhere to go,"* as Jamie Anderson beautifully expressed. But when we allow that love to guide us—when we carry it forward and honor it rather than let it anchor us in sorrow, it becomes the wind beneath our wings. Love is not meant to be locked away in the shadows of pain. It is intended to live, breathe, and be woven into our days in quiet and profound ways.

When loss leaves us broken beyond repair, when it hardens us to the beauty that remains, we risk losing not only our loved ones but also ourselves. Honoring their memory doesn't require elaborate tributes or outward displays—it's about living in a way that acknowledges the gift they will always be. Whether through simple daily rituals, quiet moments of reflection, or acts of kindness done in their name, we allow their love to continue shaping us.

Because, in the end, it is not our sorrow that binds us to them, it is our love. And love, when we let it, will always show us the way forward.

6

HOW GRIEF CHANGES THROUGH DIFFERENT RELATIONSHIPS

Grief is as unique as the love we hold for those we lose. While all loss is profound, its circumstances can shape how we grieve, face challenges, and find support. Some losses shatter the very foundation of our identity. In contrast, others leave us searching for new roles and meanings in life. The grief of a spouse, a child, or a parent is not just the loss of a person; it is the loss of a relationship that once defined us, a shared history that is woven into the fabric of our existence.

For me, the loss of my father shaped the way I would carry love and loss for the rest of my life. I was always a *daddy's girl*, bonded to my father through our shared love of sports and the lessons he instilled in me—always to try my best, never to give up. He was my foundation, my guiding force. But when I was 27, that foundation trembled beneath me. My dad was diagnosed with pancreatic cancer. Back then, the odds of surviving past a year were painfully slim, and though he fought, he lived shortly over twelve months.

I was blessed—if one can call it that in loss—to have him walk me down the aisle before he passed. I had the rare gift of leaving no word unsaid. But when he was gone, something inside me shifted. I had always believed I had time. I thought I had time to watch him become a grandfather to my children, share more milestones with him, and live in the presence of his love. And yet, time had other plans. I had no urgency to start a family before he died. Still, suddenly, the circle of life spun inside me, undeniable and profound. Six weeks after his passing, I was pregnant with Jenna.

My children never got to meet their grandfather in the way I had always dreamed. I had imagined him at every game, every event, every recital—sitting in the stands, cheering them on, the way he had always done for me. But he wasn't there, at least not in the way I had wanted.

And yet, in my heart, he never missed a thing. I have felt his presence in every moment of my children's lives, in the echoes of his wisdom guiding me, in the quiet assurance that love does not simply vanish. It shifts, transforms, and becomes something unseen yet deeply felt.

In this chapter, we explore the experience of losing a spouse, a child, a parent, a sibling, a friend, a family member, and a co-worker, offering insights into each while weaving in stories that reflect the depths of sorrow, the weight of love, and the resilience of the human heart. These stories remind us that grief is not something to conquer but something to honor. It is the evidence of love, the mark left behind by a bond that even death cannot sever. Through these pages, may you find understanding, comfort, and a recognition of your grief reflected in the experiences of others.

LOSING A SPOUSE: NAVIGATING LIFE WITHOUT YOUR PARTNER

Margaret and James spent over 35 years building a life together. They worked hard, raised their children, and reveled in the joy of watching their grandchildren grow. Their love was steady and unwavering—woven into every shared meal, whispered joke, and handheld during an evening walk. They were each other's everything. But one day, an MRI changed everything. James's headaches and blurred vision weren't just signs of aging; they were symptoms of an advanced brain tumor.

They fought. Together, they endured treatments, moments of hope, and crushing setbacks. Margaret never left his side, holding his hand through it all. But after three years, James was gone. And with him, the sweetness of their life together seemed to vanish. The laughter, the adventures, and the quiet companionship were all gone. Margaret was left in a world that no longer made sense.

For almost a year, she prayed for the end, longing to be with him despite the enormous love she had for her family, but they had their own lives now, and she didn't want to be a burden.

The bed felt too big. The house felt hollow. The absence of his voice was deafening. Without James, life had lost its color.

And then, one morning, as she sat by the window drinking coffee, she noticed the sunrise. James had always loved watching the sky shift in soft pinks and golds. That morning, for the first time in a long time, she let herself feel something other than sorrow. She let herself feel him.

It started small. She began taking morning walks, whispering to James as she walked through their favorite park. She picked up gardening again, planting the flowers he had loved most. She wrote him letters, tucking them away in a wooden box by their bed. She started having lunch with friends, sharing stories about James, and keeping him alive in her words.

And then, one day, she laughed, really laughed. And for the first time, she didn't feel guilty. Because little by little, she began to understand that loving James meant carrying him forward—not staying frozen in pain, but allowing his love to guide her into whatever life still had to offer.

Losing a spouse means learning to live in a world that no longer fits as it once did. It requires redefining who you are without them and who you are because of them. Change itself is never easy, and grief compounds the discomfort, making each step forward feel uncertain and unfamiliar. Margaret had to consciously try to fill her time in new ways, even when it felt unnatural.

Margaret still misses James every day. But now, she wakes up to the sunrise and feels his love wrapped around her. A friend invited her to play pickleball, and though Margaret initially hesitated, she accepted. She also joined a book club, finding solace in the stories and connections with others who, like her, were navigating life's transitions. In the evenings, she plays Words with Friends, a small but meaningful distraction that keeps her engaged and connected. These small actions have helped her move through life rather than remain stuck, reminding her that healing doesn't mean forgetting but learning to live again. And in doing so, she has found that love doesn't end—it simply changes form, offering us new ways to hold on, even as we move forward.

LOSING A CHILD: THE UNIMAGINABLE GRIEF OF A PARENT

No parent ever imagines outliving their child. Not only does losing a child shatter the deepest foundations of what we believe about life's natural order, but it also fractures the core of our parental identity - that primal instinct to protect our children at all costs. Through my sacred work with bereaved parents, I have walked alongside countless mothers and fathers who carry this unbearable weight. Each story is unique - some lost their precious ones to suicide, others to accidents like the one that took my daughter Jenna, and still others to the cruel hand of illness. Whether they had moments to prepare or were struck without warning, the devastating impact remains equally profound. Losing a child is a fellowship bound by profound loss, one that no parent should ever have to join.

In the raw depths of my grief after Jenna's passing, I found myself in deep spiritual contemplation. A profound question emerged: If the universe presented me with two paths - one where Jenna had never been part of my journey, sparing me this crushing pain, or another where I could hold her, love her, and be her mother, but only for fourteen precious years - which would I choose? In that sacred moment of clarity, my heart knew instantly: I would choose Jenna. I would choose every moment, every smile, every tear, every memory we shared in those fourteen years.

This revelation carries me forward even now. It's not that this understanding makes the pain disappear - nothing could ever do that. But it has transformed how I hold Jenna's life in my heart. She is not just a loss to mourn but a gift - a precious, eternal gift that changed me forever. Though her physical presence was brief, her impact on my soul is timeless. This is the perspective I've chosen to embrace: that love transcends time, that every moment with her was a blessing, and that her light continues to shine through the darkness of grief.

When parents lose a child, they enter a different dimension of existence. Time splits into before and after, and the world becomes unrecognizable. Yet, there are also the deepest and most profound forms of love in this space of profound loss. There is no roadmap through this territory of loss, no prescribed way to carry this weight. But we find ways to keep our children's spirits alive by sharing our stories, speaking our children's names, and allowing our love to flow outward even through our pain. We find ways to carry the gift forward. We learn that grief and love are not opposing forces but rather two expressions of the same profound connection - a connection that death cannot sever.

The brutal truth that losing Jenna taught me is that we don't get to control the big stuff. All those daily planners, careful schedules, and five-year plans? They're illusions of control in a world that follows its own rules. The universe doesn't ask our permission before it changes everything. But here's what I know for damn sure – while I couldn't control what happened to Jenna, I get to choose what happens next. I get to decide how her story lives on through me. That's precisely why I wrote this book – I refuse to let grief have the final word because somewhere out there, someone else needs to know they're not alone. And I've made my choice with absolute clarity: every day I draw breath; I will celebrate the gift of Jenna's life. Our love isn't just a chapter that ended – it's the force that drives me forward, the light that guides me home, and the gift that keeps giving. That's not just my choice; that's my promise.

LOSING A PARENT: THE LOSS OF HOME

In the sacred space of grief, the timing of a parent's death creates unique imprints on us. Each loss carries its profound weight, its particular ache, shaped by the moment in our life journey when this blow is severed. As we walk alongside those who grieve, we witness how the age at which one loses a parent colors not just their mourning but their very way of being in the world.

When death claims a parent in childhood, it creates a wound that touches every aspect of development. These precious ones carry an embodied absence - a space where security and guidance should have been. Their grief isn't just about missing a parent; it's about growing up feeling the absence of a parent's loving presence. They navigate life's milestones carrying questions that will never find answers, experiencing celebrations tinged with the bittersweet awareness of who isn't there to share in their joy.

Those who lose a parent in young adulthood encounter a different kind of heartbreak. Just as they begin to see their parent through adult eyes, just as the relationship begins to transform into one of mutual understanding, death intervenes. This loss often carries a particular poignancy - the grief of almost. Almost getting to know them as equals, having enough time to ask the deep questions, bridging the gap between child and adult child, nearly getting to experience them as a grandparent...almost.

When death comes to a parent in their elder years, their adult children face a complex tapestry of emotions. While society often minimizes this loss as "natural" or "expected," the reality of grief knows no such boundaries. Even after decades of connection, even with time to prepare, the death of a parent reshapes our world. Some find themselves surprised by the depth of their pain, having thought age or anticipation would cushion the blow.

The absence of a parent creates different shaped hollows in our lives. A parent is often our first experience of being fully seen and cherished, our earliest teacher in the language of love and belonging. They carry our history in their hearts - the stories of our becoming, the witness to our struggles and triumphs. When they die, we lose a complex presence that shaped us - whether through deep nurturing that served as our life's foundation or challenges that forged our resilience. For some, the loss of a parent means saying goodbye to their greatest champion and steadfast pillar of support; for others, it means confronting complicated emotions about a relationship that carried both wounds and wisdom.

Yet, in this sacred space of loss, we also witness the enduring nature of love. Whether our time with a parent was measured in years or decades, their passion becomes part of our inner landscape. Their wisdom lives on in our choices, their stories echo the tales we tell, and their presence continues moving through the world. Grief, in its profound and unrelenting nature, offers unexpected gifts. It forces us to confront life's fragility, cherish precious moments, and speak our love openly and without reservation. In the aftermath of my loss, I recently shared with my mother the profound impact she has had on the generations that followed. My daughters, I told her, possess a remarkable resilience, a strength of character that mirrors her own. Their grit and determination are a testament to the lessons she instilled in me, the unwavering love that shaped my journey. While death ends a life, it cannot sever the bonds of love that reshape us, teach us, and continue to hold us even in each other's absence.

LOSING A SIBLING: THE UNSEEN RIPPLES OF GRIEF

No one expects to lose the person who was supposed to be their witness through life, the one who knew their childhood secrets, who shared bedtime whispers, who fought with them over the front seat of the car and later stood beside them as they navigated adulthood. A sibling is often our first friend, our first rival, our first co-conspirator in the adventure of growing up. And when they are gone, it feels like an entire chapter of our story has been ripped away.

Jenna was the oldest and wore her role in our family like a second skin—strong, fierce, and unbelievably fun. She was the gravitational force that held her sisters in orbit, a protector who also pulled them into the wild adventure of her life. She was popular and loyal to her core. Jenna had a presence so magnetic that her younger sisters naturally followed her lead. They learned so much simply by being in her world—how to be brave, laugh until their stomachs hurt, and love with their whole hearts.

And then, one day, they had to learn something no child should ever have to: how to live without her.

I will never forget the moment my husband and I sat them down to tell them about Jenna's accident—that she wasn't coming home. The words shattered the air between us. Their faces crumpled, their bodies folding in on themselves in a grief too big for them to carry. They looked to us for something—some way to make sense of the impossible—but there was nothing we could give them that could undo the truth.

I have watched every step of their grief unfold.

My youngest, desperate to maintain some semblance of control in a world that had just proved itself unpredictable and cruel, developed compulsions—small rituals repeated as if she could prove her love for Jenna by getting them just right. For months, she clung to these patterns, searching for a way to make sense of the impossible. But over time, she realized that rituals do not define love—love is something she carried forward in how she lived. She learned to honor Jenna not through routines of control but by embodying the love they shared. By speaking Jenna's name, laughing the way they once had, and allowing her memory to guide her toward kindness, courage, and joy, Jenna would never be gone.

My middle daughter, suddenly thrust into the role of the eldest, stepped up in a way she never should have had to. She carried herself with grace, strength, and a quiet resilience that equally astounded and broke me. She never asked for this role, but she took it on because what else could she do? Jenna's absence created a void, and she did her best to fill it.

Losing a sibling is more than just loss, it can be a fundamental shift in identity. The person who reflected parts of you, who made sense of your childhood, who held shared memories that no one else did, is gone. And in their absence, the world tilts, forever off balance.

In the beginning, their absence is deafening. If you lost them in childhood, it is the aching space where their presence should have shaped your world, the milestones you reached without them, and the echoes of a bond that was never entirely given a chance to unfold. If you lose them in adulthood, it is the absence of the one who shared your roots, who understood the unspoken wounds and joys of your past, the only person who can reflect on your childhood like you can. Whether their loss came too soon or after years of shared history, their absence leaves a fracture in time, a loss that is both deeply personal and universally profound.

And yet, as they learn to carry grief, Jenna's presence continues to transform. Her sisters feel her in the little things. In the ritual of saying '1...2...3...JENNA' before every soccer game, in songs that bring her to mind, in inside jokes they no longer need to say aloud, and in the fierce way they love because she taught them how.

LOSING A FRIEND: THE UNSPOKEN BOND

Friendship is one of life's most profound relationships. It is love without obligation, family without blood. A true friend is someone who chooses you, who stands beside you not because they have to, but because they want to. And when they are gone, it is an ache unlike any other—the loss of a chosen bond, a trusted confidant, a keeper of our best and worst moments.

Samantha and Olivia met in college and were inseparable from the start. They navigated heartbreaks together, celebrated each other's triumphs, and dreamed about growing old as friends who drank wine on front porches and laughed until they cried. When Olivia was diagnosed with cancer, Samantha never let her see the fear in her eyes. She held her hand through the most challenging days, never once believing a world without Olivia could exist.

But then it did.

Samantha reached for her phone instinctively, only to remember there would be no reply. Every milestone, every funny story, every moment she would have shared with Olivia now sat heavy in her chest. She didn't just lose her best friend—she lost the person who knew her heart inside and out. Olivia just *got* her in a way few ever had. She listened like not many people do, with an openness that made Samantha feel truly seen. She validated her feelings, dreams, and fears—never dismissing, judging, just *understanding*. And now, without Olivia, the world felt lonelier, as if a crucial piece of her had gone missing, one that could never be replaced.

For a long time, it felt like nothing could fill the space Olivia left behind. And maybe nothing ever honestly could. But one day, Samantha said something Olivia would have said, making a joke she knew her friend would love. And for the first time, it felt like Olivia was still there—not just in memory, but in the whispers of her presence woven into their unbreakable bond. In the way she caught herself thinking *Olivia would have loved this*, in the sudden warmth of an inside joke only the two of them would have understood, in the quiet moments when she could almost hear Olivia's voice. It wasn't the same, but it was something—something that reminded her that Olivia was somehow still here.

Losing a friend means losing a piece of the world that made sense. So many people go through life never genuinely feeling heard or validated, but a true friend sees you in a way others don't. They listen—not just to your words, but to what's beneath them. They are not in competition with you; instead, they are your greatest cheerleader, celebrating your wins as if they were their own and holding space for your pain without judgment. When they are gone, you miss more than just their presence, you miss the way they made you feel understood, supported, and deeply valued. Their absence leaves a silence that is hard to fill, not just because they are gone, but because the kind of love they gave is rare, and its loss is immeasurable. But just as they stood by you in life, their love and presence can continue to shape you in their absence.

LOSING A FAMILY MEMBER: THE THREADS THAT BIND US

Losing a family member is more than just saying goodbye—it is the unraveling of a thread in the intricate quilt we call family, a piece of color and warmth that once made the fabric whole. Whether it is the wisdom of a grandparent, the light of a grandchild, the laughter of an uncle, the nurturing presence of an aunt, the companionship of a cousin, or the boundless joy of a niece or nephew, each loss alters the landscape of our lives. Family is complicated. It is love, history, and tradition; sometimes, it is complex and messy. But no matter what, family shapes us.

Javier grew up in a tight-knit family, where they treated Sunday dinners as sacred and celebrated every milestone together. His mother's brother, Uncle Emilio, was his greatest mentor, the one who taught him how to fish, who showed up to every game, who believed in him when he didn't believe in himself. When Emilio passed unexpectedly, the grief felt insurmountable.

At first, his absences were everywhere. It was in the empty chair at the dinner table, in the jokes no one else told in quite the same way, in the voicemail messages Javier couldn't bear to delete. Javier returned to the places Uncle Emilio and he shared—the pier where they had spent countless afternoons and the diner where Uncle Emilio always ordered the same thing. He couldn't fathom a world where his uncle wasn't just a phone call away.

For those who lose a grandparent, it can feel like losing a pillar of strength, the one who was the bedrock of the family unit and giver of unconditional love. For those who lose a cousin, it can feel like losing the friend who understood you before the world told you who to be. The loss of a grandchild is unbearable—not just because of your grief, but because you must also witness the deep, unrelenting sorrow of your child's grief. It is a double layer of heartbreak, an ache that extends in both directions.

For those who lose a niece or nephew, grief carries a different weight. It is the pain of watching a life cut short, of knowing all the love and guidance you wanted to offer will now go unspoken. But even more heartbreaking is witnessing your sibling—a brother or sister you've known your whole life—carry the unbearable weight of losing their child. You see their world shatter in ways words cannot reach, and you feel powerless to take even a fraction of their pain away.

You grieve for the life that ended too soon and for the one that intertwined with yours for decades. And you grieve the absence of a steady presence, the wisdom of a grandparent who had always been there, the gentle guidance of an older sibling, the unwavering support of an aunt or uncle who knew just what to say.

You ache for the laughter that should have filled the years ahead, the treasured stories they will never tell again, and the moments that now exist only in memory. At the same time, you grieve for those left behind—the parents who have lost a child, the siblings who have lost a lifelong companion, and the spouses who must now navigate a future they never imagined facing alone. Whether their time was beginning, or they had spent a lifetime shaping yours, their absence leaves a void that cannot be filled, a love that must now be carried forward in a different way.

Every loss within a family reshapes its dynamic, but love is never truly lost. It lives on in the traditions we continue, the recipes we pass down through generations, the stories we share around the dinner table, and the small, everyday moments where we still feel their presence. Though grief may change how we gather, it does not erase the bonds that connect us. And just like a quilt, where one piece ends, another can attach. Their love, their influence, and their presence create space for new connections, for deeper relationships to form, and for the family to continue growing while always carrying them within its design.

It took time, but eventually, Javier realized something profound: Emilio wasn't truly gone. His lessons lived on in the way Javier taught his own son to fish, in the wisdom he shared, in the way he loved fiercely and fully. Grief had shifted, but love remained.

Losing a family member, whether expected or sudden, leaves a void. Still, their love continues through the beautiful and sometimes messy quilt we call family. Their thread never lost—it weaves into us, becoming part of our fabric.

LOSING A CO-WORKER: THE QUIET ABSENCE IN THE WORKPLACE

A workplace is more than just a job. It is a community where we spend a significant portion of our lives. Over time, colleagues become more than just people we work with—they become our morning coffee companions, sounding boards, and trusted allies in the daily grind. When a co-worker passes away, the loss is often understated yet deeply felt.

Tom had worked alongside Ben for nearly a decade. Together, they made work more than just a place to clock in and out—they made it fun. They organized the annual Super Bowl pool, turning it into a full-fledged office event with ridiculous prizes, like a golden football trophy that no one wanted, but everyone fought to win. They set up March Madness brackets, hosted impromptu trivia contests during lunch breaks, and were the masterminds behind the legendary "Ugly Holiday Sweater Showdown," where Ben once wore a sweater so obnoxious it lit up and played music.

Ben was the first person to greet Tom every morning, who knew exactly how he took his coffee, the steady force in an often chaotic office. When he passed away unexpectedly, the office felt hollow. The missing laughter, the absence of his daily check-ins—it all felt surreal.

The first team meeting without him was the hardest. Someone else sat in his chair, but no one could fill his place. There was an unspoken grief in the office, a shared understanding that Ben had been more than just a colleague—he had been part of the heartbeat of their workplace.

Tom found solace in small acts—keeping a framed photo of Ben at his desk, organizing a charity event in his honor, and continuing the traditions they had started together. The Super Bowl pool was different without Ben's sarcastic commentary. However, Tom still ran it, knowing Ben would have wanted the fun to continue. His influence remained; woven into the culture he had helped create.

Losing a co-worker may not come with the same rituals of mourning as losing a family member, but it is a profound loss nonetheless. It is the absence of a familiar presence, a missing piece of the daily routine. And yet, the impact of their kindness, humor, and work ethic lingers in the echoes of the workplace they helped shape.

Loss comes in many forms, each carrying its weight, lessons, and transformation. But through every loss, one truth remains: love never disappears. It changes shape, finds new expressions, and it continues to guide us forward.

THE SHAPE OF GRIEF, THE SHAPE OF LOVE

Grief is as varied as the relationships that define our lives. Each loss carries a distinction, not just because of who we have lost but because of who we were with them. A spouse, a child, a parent, a sibling, a family member, a friend, or a colleague captures a different part of our hearts, shaping our identity, sense of belonging, and how we move through the world. When they are gone, it is not just their presence we mourn but their specific role in our lives and the irre-placeable imprint they left behind.

Losing a spouse unravels a shared life and breaks a partnership meant to last a lifetime. It leaves behind a hollow space where companionship once lived. The loss of a child is an unspeakable fracture, a violation of the natural order, an ache that stretches beyond words. A parent's death feels like the loss of home itself—the witness to our beginnings, the keeper of our history. The death of a family member disrupts the foundation of our lives, removing a presence that shapes our memories, traditions, and sense of belonging. A sibling's absence is the severing of a bond that tethered us to childhood, a connection that no one else can quite replicate. The loss of a close friend strips us of the one who chose us, who understood us in a way that felt effortless. Even the passing of a co-worker, though often minimized, can shake the very rhythm of our daily lives, leaving behind a silence where laughter and camaraderie once existed.

No two griefs are the same because no two loves are the same. Each relationship shapes us in unique ways, and so too does its loss. Some griefs roar like a tidal wave; others seep like a slow, quiet tide. Some make us feel unconnected, lost in the vastness of what was, while others leave us searching for meaning in what remains. But all grief, whether explosive or quiet, sharp or lingering—reflects love.

This is why grief is not something we "move on" from. We carry it because we carry love. And though loss changes us, so too does love. It stretches, transforms, and finds its way into new spaces if we allow it—not to replace what was lost but to remind us that love is never truly gone. It lingers in the stories we tell, the habits we keep, the gifts they bestowed upon our lives, and how we live because of who they were to us. I like to think of them as our forever gifts.

Grief is not just about the absence of someone we love, it is about the presence of that love, reshaped but never erased. The people who have passed before us are still with us, woven into the fabric of who we are. And if grief is the price of love, then let it be a price we pay with tenderness, with remembrance, with a heart forever filled with gratitude, and shaped by those we have loved.

7
ADDRESSING GUILT AND REGRET

The moment they told him, his breath left his body. It was not just grief that swallowed him whole—it was something darker, heavier: guilt. The kind that clings to your ribs settles deep in your bones and whispers the same questions repeatedly: *What if I had done something differently? What if I had seen it coming? What if...*

He should have known. He should have done more.

Leah had always been the kind of person who carried everyone else's burdens without complaint. She was the friend who showed up unannounced with coffee when you were having a bad day and remembered the small details that made you feel seen. Leah made people believe everything would be okay, even when her world was falling apart. And somewhere along the way, no one—not even him—noticed how much she was carrying alone.

It had been a challenging year. First, Leah lost her job. Then, her apartment. One thing after another, until it seemed like nothing in her life was steady. But Leah was resilient and headstrong. She made jokes about it and brushed off concern with a casual, *I'll figure it out, don't worry.* And he believed her.

The night before she died, she called him. It was late, and he was exhausted. He let it go to voicemail. *I'll call her back in the morning,* he told himself. But morning never came for Leah.

He replays that night over and over in his head. What if he had picked up? What if he had asked the right questions? Would she still be here? Could he have been the one thing that made her stay?

No one has answers for him. They say the things they think will help. *It was not your fault. You couldn't have known. Leah made her own choice.* But those words do nothing to silence the relentless ache of *if only.*

Grief on its own is unbearable. But grief wrapped in guilt? That is a weight that suffocates.

For weeks, he sat in the quiet, letting it consume him. He stopped answering messages. He avoided the places they used to go. He couldn't even bring himself to say Leah's name without breaking. Because speaking her name meant acknowledging that she was *gone,* and what was left of him if she was gone?

Then, one night, he found her last voicemail. He had almost deleted it without listening, afraid of what he might hear. But he pressed play, his hands trembling. Her voice was soft, almost steady. "*Hey, I just... I don't know. I just wanted to talk. It's been a rough one, you know?* A pause. *Anyway, call me when you get a chance. No pressure, just... yeah.*"

That was it. Nothing desperate, nothing final. Just Leah, reaching out. And he hadn't been there.

He wanted to stay in that moment forever, punishing himself for not answering. But grief has a strange way of shifting, of making room for something else. As he listened to her voice again and again, he heard something new—an invitation not to drown in guilt but to carry her forward in a way that mattered.

She had spent her life showing up for people, and perhaps the best way to honor Leah was to do the same.

The weight of guilt does not vanish overnight. It lingers, softening at the edges, reshaping itself into something different. But it no longer owns him. He has learned to sit with it, listen to it, and let it move through him when he is ready. Not because he forgets but because love demands more of him than self-punishment because she would want him to remember her with laughter, not regret. Because maybe, just maybe, the best way to honor the ones we lose is to keep living —not in their absence, but in the love they left behind.

NAVIGATING GUILT AND REGRET: A PERSONAL TOOLKIT

This toolkit is designed to help you navigate the weight of guilt and regret in a way that fosters healing rather than self-punishment. These emotions, while painful, often arise from the deep love and responsibility we felt for the person we lost. But carrying the weight of guilt and regret indefinitely does not honor that love, it only keeps us stuck. Through reflection, self-compassion, and intentional practices, you can begin to loosen their grip, not by ignoring them, but by understanding them. This is not about erasing the past; it is about making peace with it, practicing forgiveness—both for yourself and for the circumstances beyond your control—and allowing yourself to move forward while still holding on to the love that remains.

1. Acknowledge Your Feelings with Reflection

Find a quiet space, take a few deep breaths, and allow yourself to sit with your emotions. Before you begin, consider whether you would feel more supported by having a trusted friend, therapist, or grief counselor available to talk through anything that comes up.

Although your grief is deeply personal, you do not have to navigate it alone.

When you feel ready, write down specific thoughts or situations that evoke guilt or regret. For each one, ask yourself:

- *What was within my control, and what was not?*
- *What do I understand about my intentions, and what influenced them throughout these circumstances?*
- *If a dear friend were in my position, what guidance might I offer them?*

If you feel overwhelmed at any point, pause. Try a grounding exercise—such as placing your feet firmly on the ground, focusing on your breath, or naming things you can see and hear around you—to help bring yourself back to the present moment.

This exercise is not meant to reinforce guilt but to help you clarify the origins of these emotions and guide you toward a more compassionate understanding of yourself. If, at any point, the emotions feel too heavy to carry alone, please consider reaching out for professional support. Healing is not about processing everything at once but permitting yourself to move through it at your own pace, with care and support.

2. Practice Self-Compassion

Treat yourself with the same kindness and understanding you would offer a close friend.

Remind yourself:

- *I am human and fallible, and my actions were shaped by my understanding at the time—even if, looking back, I now see things differently.*

- *It is normal to feel guilt and regret, but I do not have to be defined by them.*
- *I can acknowledge these emotions without letting them consume me.*

Allow yourself the grace to move through these feelings rather than stay trapped in them indefinitely.

3. Speak Your Guilt and Regret Aloud

Guilt and regret thrive in silence, feeding on the mind's tendency to ruminate—looping painful thoughts repeatedly without resolution. The more we replay these moments, the more the mind fabricates and dramatizes its version of events, often distorting reality and reinforcing narratives of self-blame that may not be grounded in truth. Carl Jung once said, *"Until you make the unconscious conscious, it will direct your life, and you will call it fate."* When left unchecked, rumination strengthens our most profound forms of guilt and regret rather than revealing clarity. Their power grows when kept in secrecy, making it harder to find perspective. By expressing them—whether to a trusted friend, a counselor, or through healthy outlets—you begin to interrupt that cycle, stripping away their hold and creating space for clarity and healing.

Here are some additional options beyond journaling and talking to someone who can help constructively process guilt and regret:

- **Engage in a Creative Outlet** – Sometimes, emotions are too heavy for words. Try expressing them through painting, music, poetry, or movement (like dance or mindful walking). Creativity can provide a release that words cannot.
- **Practice Mindfulness and Meditation** – Mindfulness techniques help ground you in the present moment, reducing the spiral of self-blame. Guided meditations

focused on self-compassion can be particularly helpful in loosening the grip of guilt.

- **Write a Letter (Without Sending It)** – If unresolved feelings or words are left unsaid, write a letter to your loved one. Express everything on your heart. Whether you keep, burn, or tuck it away, this exercise can help externalize emotions and bring a sense of release.
- **Engage in Acts of Service** – Redirecting painful emotions into meaningful action can create a sense of purpose. Volunteering, helping others, or supporting a cause your loved one cared about can transform grief into connection.
- **Use Movement to Process Emotion** – The body holds grief just as much as the mind. Gentle yoga, walking in nature, or even something more intense like running or boxing can help move heavy emotions through the body, providing relief.
- **Symbolic Rituals or Memorial Practices** – Create a ritual to honor your loved one and release guilt. This could be listening to their favorite upbeat music, planting a tree, or visiting a place that was meaningful to them. Sometimes, tangible acts help externalize internal emotions.
- **Listen to an Audiobook for Perspective** – When guilt feels overwhelming, hearing the wisdom of others can shift your perspective. Choose an audiobook on self-compassion, grief, or personal growth to help reframe negative self-talk, offer guidance on healing, and remind you that you are not alone in your experience.

4. Understand That Healing is Nonlinear

As discussed in other sections of this book, the journey through grief is rarely linear, and the same applies to guilt and regret. Some days, these emotions will soften, allowing space for peace and joy. Other days, they may return unexpectedly, like a sudden wind stirring up embers you thought had cooled, catching you off guard with their sting. This ebb and flow is natural and does not mean you are moving backward—only that grief, like fire, can smolder beneath the surface and flare up when least expected.

When difficult emotions arise, remind yourself that while they may feel overwhelming, they do not have to be permanent. You can guide these emotions with intention and self-compassion rather than let them consume you. Develop an awareness of your triggers and prepare ways to ground yourself when they appear. And most importantly, allow space for joy without guilt—experiencing moments of peace or happiness does not diminish the depth of your love or grief. Healing does not mean forgetting; it means learning to carry love and loss side by side.

Here are some strategies to help navigate the nonlinear path of emotions when they arise:

- **Practice Grounding Techniques** – Use deep breathing, sensory awareness (naming things you see, hear, feel), or holding a physical object to anchor yourself in the present moment. These techniques can help loosen the grip of the overwhelming thoughts born in the past.
- **Shift Your Environment**—When emotions feel overwhelming, step outside for fresh air, walk, or change rooms to create a physical reset.
- **Engage in a Soothing Activity** – Listen to calming music, take a warm bath, journal, or do something creative to redirect your focus.
- **Use a Comforting Affirmation** – Repeat phrases like *"I did the best I could with what I knew at the time"* or *"I can hold both sorrow and self-compassion in the same space."*
- **Visualize a Safe Space** – Imagine where you feel at peace— whether it is a childhood home, a beach, or a quiet forest— and mentally transport yourself there.

- **Talk to Someone You Trust -** If your emotions feel too heavy to carry alone, reach out to a friend, therapist, or support group.
- **Allow Yourself to Feel Joy Without Guilt** – Remember that experiencing happiness does not mean forgetting your loved one; you are honoring their love by continuing to live.
- **Prepare a Self-Compassionate Response to Triggers** – If certain dates, places, or experiences intensify grief, plan ahead by deciding how to care for yourself when those moments arise.
- **Create a Ritual to Acknowledge Your Loved One** – Do something in their honor, visit a meaningful place, or speak their name when emotions surface to channel your feelings into connection rather than distress.

These strategies do not erase pain, but they help ease its weight, allowing you to hold both love and loss in a way that fosters healing and growth.

5. Integrate, Rather Than Erase, Guilt and Regret

Healing does not entirely eliminate guilt and regret—it is about learning to hold them without letting them consume you. These emotions reflect the depth of your love, but they do not have to define your life, unravel your happiness, or keep you from moving forward. Your journey continues, and with intention and self-compassion, you can honor your grief while still creating space for joy, meaning, and growth.

- **Let them be reminders of how deeply you cared** – Your guilt and regret exist because your love was profound. Acknowledge that they stem from your connection's depth, not failure.
- **Allow them to shape your choices moving forward** – Use

this experience to bring greater awareness, empathy, and intention into your relationships and decisions.

- **Reflect on what you've learned** – Consider how this experience has changed you. What insights have you gained about love, loss, and resilience?
- **Find ways to share these lessons** – Whether through supporting others, deepening your connections, or simply living with more presence, let what you've learned guide you.
- **Trust that the weight will shift** – Guilt and regret will soften over time. What will remain is love—not just loss.

Above all, be gentle with yourself. Healing is an ongoing practice of allowing love, grief, guilt, and regret to coexist without letting them overshadow the light of your loved one's presence in your life. The greatest way to honor them is to live fully—not despite your loss, but because their love is still a part of you. Your life matters and moving forward does not mean leaving them behind; it means carrying them with you as you create a life that reflects the depth of the love you shared. Their love has shaped you, and if you choose, it can make you even more compassionate, present, and intentional in how you live. Through you, their love continues to touch the world, making it a better place in their honor.

BRENDAN'S STORY: THE WEIGHT OF WHAT-IFS

Brendan had always been the kind of father who showed up. He made it to every recital and every competition he could, cheering from the audience with his phone in hand, ready to capture every moment. But this time, Brendan wasn't there. He had a work obligation, one that felt too important to miss. The Sales Kickoff event had been on his calendar for months, and the dinner the night before was crucial—a meeting that could seal the deal on a major account he had been nurturing for nearly a year.

The night before Mariah and the girls left, he came home late, exhausted but hopeful about the deal. He glanced at his sleeping wife and daughters as he got into bed, thinking he would see them in a few days. In the morning, he did his best to be quiet, not wanting to wake them as he slipped out the door. He figured they would connect later.

But later never came.

When he landed in Chicago, his bag was so badly damaged that he had to stop and file a claim at baggage services. When he finished, he realized he had missed Mariah's call. She left a voicemail, her voice light but hurried, telling him they were about to get on the road and she'd call him back when they stopped. He texted her, "Drive safe. Love you," before heading to his hotel.

When she called him back, he did not hear his phone ring. He was caught up in a conversation with a colleague about some client issue —something that felt important at the time but now seemed so insignificant that it made him sick. When he called her back, the call went straight to voicemail. He tried again: nothing.

Hours later, he was in a strategy session when his phone rang again. This time, it wasn't Mariah. It was a number he didn't recognize. He let it go to voicemail.

The caller left a voicemail. The transcription on his screen was chilling in its simplicity:

"This is Officer Cutright. Please call me back at..."

Brendan stared at the words; his mind unable to process them. His body went cold, a slow numbness creeping in as if his brain refused to let meaning take hold. His hands shook as he stepped out of the meeting room, his legs unsteady. He barely registered the murmur of voices behind him, the way his colleagues glanced at him with mild curiosity as he walked toward the hallway.

His fingers fumbled over the screen as he dialed the number—the call connected on the first ring.

"This is Officer Cutright," a steady voice answered.

Brendan swallowed hard. *"This is Brendan Lawson. You called me." His voice felt foreign, distant,* like it belonged to someone else.

There was a pause. Then, the officer's voice softened. *"Mr. Lawson, I am so sorry to tell you this. Your wife, Mariah, and your daughters, Skyler and Dakota, were in an accident on the interstate. A semi-truck came to a sudden stop. There was no time to react. They,"* the officer hesitated, *"They didn't make it."*

The words didn't land at first. They floated in the air, distant and unreal.

"No," Brendan whispered.

The officer continued speaking about the next steps, arrangements, and identification. But Brendan couldn't hear any of it. His ears rang, and his vision blurred. The phone slipped from his hand and hit the floor with a dull thud.

Somewhere, someone was calling his name. A hand touched his arm. He turned, but all he saw was movement, colors, and shapes that no longer made sense.

Brendan's world had shattered. And he was standing in the wreckage, unable to move, unable to breathe, unable to make it all stop.

Brendan did not remember how he got out of the conference room, only that at some point, he was on the floor in the hotel hallway, his chest caving in with grief. The hours after were a blur. He booked the next flight home, barely able to see through the haze of shock and disbelief.

Then came the guilt.

Why didn't I wake them before I left? Why didn't I kiss them goodbye?

Why did I waste time filing that stupid baggage claim?

Why didn't I answer when she called?

Why wasn't I with them?

The questions looped in his mind like a cruel, endless cycle, playing out every possible way he could have changed the outcome. Had he been there, he may have been the one driving. He may have taken a different route. Maybe he could have somehow prevented it. He tortured himself with these thoughts as if his absence had somehow set the tragedy in motion.

For months, regret consumed Brendan. He withdrew from everyone, isolating himself in the house that no longer felt like home. His world became small and silent, haunted by what-ifs. He replayed their last moments repeatedly, trying to recall the last words he had spoken to them. He couldn't remember. He had been rushing and preoccupied.

That realization crushed him.

At night, he barely slept. When he did, he dreamed of them, only to wake up to the unbearable reality of their absence. The house, once filled with laughter and music from the girls practicing their routines, was suffocating in its stillness.

LEARNING TO LIVE WITH THE UNTHINKABLE

Brendan's grief counselor told him something that, at first, made him angry. *"You did not cause this, Brendan."*

But that is not how it felt. Everything—every choice he made in those last hours—had led to that outcome.

Over time, through therapy and support groups, Brendan started to see the truth of what his counselor was saying. Guilt gave him the illusion of control, believing he could have changed the outcome if he had done something different. But that was not reality. The accident was not his fault. The universe was not waiting for him to make the right or wrong move to determine their fate.

Brendan was not ready to forgive himself, but he was willing to learn how to carry his grief differently.

He began to write letters to Mariah, Skyler, and Dakota—letters filled with the things he wished he had said, the moments he wished he could relive. He started running in the early mornings, pushing his body to exhaustion to get out of his head for a little while. He went back to work, though nothing about it felt the same.

One night, months after the accident, he sat in the girls' empty dance room, staring at the trophies representing their hard work. And for the first time, he asked himself a new question: *What would Mariah want for me? What would Skyler and Dakota want?* The answer was not to stay buried in guilt or keep punishing himself for something he had no power to change. They would want him to keep living, to find joy again—not to erase the loss but to carry their love forward.

A BRIDGE TO FORGIVENESS

Brendan's story reminds us that guilt and regret, when left unchecked, can become prisons. They can make us believe we are responsible for things beyond our control, keeping us locked in the past we cannot change. But in time and with intention, we can choose to carry our grief in a way that honors the love we will always share rather than drowning in the weight of what-ifs.

Forgiveness, especially self-forgiveness, is not about erasing the past. It is about making peace with it. The next section of this chapter will explore what it means to take that step—not because the pain disappears, but because we deserve to carry our grief with love rather than self-punishment. If guilt has become the language of your grief, let's explore how to rewrite it in a way that moves you forward with love as your guiding light—not to forget but to heal.

PATHWAYS TO FORGIVENESS: A PRACTICAL GUIDE

When grief lingers like an uninvited guest, guilt, and regret can feel impossible to release. Forgiving yourself is not about excusing the past or pretending it did not happen—it is about loosening the grip of self-blame and making space for healing. It is about recognizing that you made choices with the best knowledge and resources you had at the time. This realization may feel both liberating and overwhelming, but freeing yourself from the chains of guilt is essential.

Forgiveness is not a single act, it is a practice that requires intention, patience, and self-compassion. These exercises are designed to help you shift from self-punishment to self-understanding. They allow you to integrate the lessons of your experience while releasing the pain that no longer serves you or enabling you to celebrate your loved one who has passed.

SELF-REFLECTION: ASKING THE RIGHT QUESTIONS

To begin the process of self-forgiveness, take a moment to pause and reflect. Find a quiet space, take a deep breath, and consider the following:

- What specific moments or choices make me feel guilty?
- What were the circumstances influencing my decisions at that time?
- What did I not know then that I understand now?
- If someone I love were in my position, how would I respond to them?

- How have I allowed guilt and regret to shape my life since my loss?
- In what ways have I honored my loved one despite my pain?

Our minds seek patterns, assign meaning, and create narratives to make sense of the world around us. This cognitive process, known as *causal attribution*, is a fundamental part of interpreting life events. When faced with loss, particularly one that is sudden or traumatic, the brain scrambles to fill in the gaps, searching for a reason, something or someone to hold responsible. Often, that blame turns inward.

Psychological research supports this. A study by Janoff-Bulman (1979) on *assumptive world theory* found that when people experience a life-altering event, their pre-existing beliefs about safety, fairness, and predictability shatter. To regain control, they unconsciously create simplified explanations for what happened—ones that often distort reality. Similarly, research on *counterfactual thinking* (Roese & Olson, 1995) shows that the mind frequently plays out "if only" and "what if" scenarios, convincing us that a different action could have changed the outcome. These mental loops intensify guilt, making us believe we have more power over a situation than we truly do.

These questions are not meant to assign blame but to help you untangle the story guilt has told you about yourself. Often, guilt thrives on a simplified, distorted storyline that roars within you, suggesting you had more control than you actually did. But our minds are imperfect storytellers, and when we step back, we can begin to recognize the whole picture. By looking deeper, you allow yourself to see the complexity of what happened—not just in hindsight, but with the clarity of truth rather than the distortion of guilt. Understanding this cognitive tendency can be the first step toward releasing the weight of self-blame and moving toward a more compassionate perspective.

SELF-FORGIVENESS LETTER

Writing a self-forgiveness letter is one of the most powerful ways to process and release guilt. Writing this letter is not about perfect words or structured sentences—it is about speaking to yourself with the kindness you would offer a grieving friend. It is about becoming increasingly aware of the thoughts and feelings guiding you now, acknowledging their weight without letting them define your future. Through this self-discovery practice, you can shift your focus from regret to the enduring love you will always share. By permitting yourself to grieve with compassion, you create space for healing— not by letting go of your loved one, but by carrying them forward in a way that honors both their memory and your journey ahead.

1. Begin by addressing yourself with empathy. Acknowledge the pain you carry.
2. Write about the specific moments that have caused you guilt. Let the words flow without judgment.
3. Express understanding of your choices at the time, recognizing the context in which you made them.
4. Offer yourself the compassion you would extend to someone in your shoes.
5. End with an affirmation of your humanity and a commitment to moving forward.

You may not believe the words at first. That is okay. Writing them is an act of courage. Over time, as you revisit this letter, you may begin to see yourself with more compassion.

RELEASING GUILT THROUGH VISUALIZATION

Psychologists have long studied the tendency for people to hold onto guilt as a form of self-punishment or as a misguided way to express devotion to a lost loved one. This phenomenon, often linked to *moral self-injury* or *survivor's guilt*, can create a false sense of obligation—an unconscious belief that by carrying guilt, one is proving one's love, loyalty, or grief.

A study by Kubany and Manke (1995) on *guilt and cognitive distortions* found that many individuals believe releasing guilt is equivalent to forgetting or dishonoring the person they lost. This *self-imposed suffering* is a cognitive distortion, reinforcing the belief that punishment is necessary for atonement. However, research in grief therapy (Neimeyer, 2001) suggests that true healing does not come from self-punishment but from finding ways to *integrate love and loss into one's life with meaning and purpose.*

If guilt has become a constant voice in your mind, visualization can help shift the grip it has over you. But for some, visualizing release—like placing guilt into a river—can feel like a betrayal, as if letting go means letting go of the person they lost. If this resonates with you, consider reframing the visualization. Instead of picturing guilt floating away, imagine transforming it. See it dissolving into light, shifting into something that carries your love forward rather than moving you away from your loved one. Imagine your loved one touching your shoulder, gently reassuring you that you do not need to suffer to prove your love.

- **Picture a friend coming to you, carrying the same guilt you feel now.** Imagine their sorrow, their regret, their pain. What would you say to them? How would you reassure them?
- **Now, reverse the roles.** See yourself in their place. Allow yourself to receive the exact words of kindness and forgiveness.
- **If fully letting go feels too difficult, visualize an alternative.**
  - Imagine your guilt dissolving into light, transforming into warmth and love surrounding your body.

- ○ Picture your loved one guiding you toward peace, reassuring you that suffering is not proof of love.
- ○ **Redirect your guilt into a tangible symbol of love and remembrance.** Use a candle, a flower, a stone, or another object as a sign of your love. Let this symbol serve as a reminder that your connection endures, not through pain, but through the love and memories you continue to honor.
- **Redirect your guilt into action.** If you struggle with the idea of release, consider shifting it into something tangible:
  - ○ Perform an act of kindness in your loved one's honor.
  - ○ Start a ritual or tradition that keeps their memory alive.
  - ○ Allow yourself to live fully, not as an act of forgetting, but as a way of carrying their presence forward and living the best life possible in their honor.

This practice allows you to see yourself differently, moving away from the rigid, self-critical lens that guilt often imposes. By choosing to carry love instead of guilt, you are not letting go of them, you are allowing their presence to guide you in a way that brings light into your world again as a symbol of your undying love.

DAILY ACTS OF SELF-FORGIVENESS

Healing does not happen in a single moment—we build it through our small, daily choices to be gentler with ourselves. Consider incorporating the following into your daily life:

- **Speak kindness to yourself.** Replace guilt-driven thoughts with affirmations like: *I did the best I could in that moment.*
- **Engage in movement.** Physical activity, whether walking, yoga, or even stretching—can help shift emotional weight.
- **Practice mindful breathing.** When guilt resurfaces, pause. Take a deep breath in for four counts, hold for four, and

release for four. Remember that emotions are meant to move through you, not consume you.

- **Find an outlet for expression.** Art, music, and storytelling can be powerful ways to process and release emotions that feel too complex or overwhelming for everyday words alone.
- **Give back in a way that honors your loved one.** Channel your love and grief into something meaningful—volunteering, creating, and supporting others who are struggling.

FORGIVENESS AS A JOURNEY, NOT A DESTINATION

Self-forgiveness does not mean forgetting, nor does it mean minimizing the weight of your choices. It means recognizing that guilt does not define you, nor should it dictate your future. When you hold onto guilt, you allow it to take up space within you—space that could be filled with love, purpose, and connection.

Some days, guilt will feel lighter. On other days, it may surge back with force. But each time you choose self-compassion over self-punishment, you reclaim a piece of yourself. You open a door for healing, making space for the love, the lessons, and the life that still awaits you. Forgiveness is not about erasing the past; it is about allowing light to return so you can turn around and share it with the world.

I like to think this light is the light of our loved ones. They do not want us to live in darkness. They want us to continue—to carry them forward in how we live, love, and give. As you continue this journey, remind yourself: Forgiveness is not something you earn—it is something you choose. And every time you choose it, you take another step toward healing, honoring your love for them, acknowledging how they blessed your life, and bringing their light into the world.

8

BUILDING SUPPORTIVE
NETWORKS

We've walked this path together long enough to know—grief is heavy, and it can feel impossibly isolating. I don't need to tell you that; you've lived it. You've carried its weight, felt its silence, and wrestled with its unpredictability. But as we've explored throughout these pages, grief is not meant to be endured alone.

I didn't know where to turn in the early days after Jenna's passing. The thought of walking into a room full of grieving people felt unbearable. I wasn't ready to speak my pain out loud, to sit in a circle and hear reflections of my sorrow in the voices of others.

But grief can bring people into your life exactly when you need them. For me, that person was Kathryn.

She was the grandmother of one of Jenna's best friends, and she had been offering grief counseling through her missionary work for years. Usually, she waited three weeks before reaching out to a grieving family, giving them time to catch their breath in the suffocating fog of loss. But with us, she felt compelled to come sooner. I will always be grateful that she did.

In those first days, I needed someone who could sit with me in my grief, who could see the weight I was carrying and offer something— not to fix it, but to help me bear it. Kathryn did precisely that.

One morning, she suggested a guided relaxation session. I agreed, not knowing what to expect, only knowing that I would try anything to ease the pain that had rooted itself so deeply inside me.

I lay down, closed my eyes, and followed her voice as she led me into deep stillness. With every breath, I let go just enough to allow my body to soften, to release the tension I hadn't even realized I was holding. Then, she asked me to picture a staircase—one of my designs. Step by step, I descended, the noise of my grief quieting ever so slightly with each count.

At the bottom, she asked me to step into the most beautiful place I had ever been. Instantly, my mind transported me to Oahu, the breathtaking Kaneohe Klipper Golf Course cliffs, where the Pacific stretched endlessly before me. I could feel the warm breeze against my skin and hear the rhythmic crash of the waves below.

Then, she invited me to call forth someone I loved.

Without hesitation, I whispered to my father. I ached for his presence, for the comfort of his steady voice. And suddenly, he was there. He was just as I remembered him—his tan Dockers, his perfectly combed silver hair, his grounding and familiar presence. I barely had time to absorb the moment before he turned and led me toward a brilliant light.

And there she was, Jenna.

Her golden locks framed her face, her hazel eyes bright and full of understanding. She didn't speak, not in words, but I felt her love wrap around me, holding me up when I felt like crumbling. I wanted to stay in that moment forever. I wanted to ask her everything—*Why did you have to go? How do I survive this? How do I carry this pain? How does our family move on without you?*

But then, Kathryn's voice called me back. It was time to return.

I didn't want to leave, but I knew I had to. As my father guided Jenna away, she shifted back into pure light. I climbed the staircase, each step pulling me further from them. When I finally opened my eyes, I felt the ache of goodbye again. But I also felt something else—I felt her.

That moment didn't take away my grief. It didn't erase my pain. But it showed me that love doesn't disappear. Even in depths of sorrow, I was not alone.

In those early days, Kathryn became my support system. Her steady presence helped me keep my footing when the ground felt crumbling beneath me.

Many months later, when I finally walked into a bereavement group, I carried that experience with me. By then, I had learned that healing doesn't happen in isolation. I have seen firsthand that people are willing to sit with you in your pain to remind you that you are not alone. Some of my closest friends and family members had already sought the comfort of a grief group just weeks after Jenna passed, but I wasn't ready then. When I finally did attend, I understood why they had gone.

This chapter is about finding those connections. Whether through a single person like Kathryn, a circle of friends who understand, or a structured group offering support, we heal together. While grief is deeply personal, loss is part of the human experience, and we are not meant to walk the path forward alone.

FINDING THE SUPPORT THAT FEELS RIGHT

In the days, weeks, and months after loss, seeking support can feel like another impossible task. You may not even know what you need, and the idea of reaching out—of putting words to something so unspeakable—can be overwhelming. I understand that hesitation. After Jenna passed, Kathryn arrived like a steady presence, offering her quiet wisdom without expectation. I wasn't ready for a grief group then, but when I was, it became another source of comfort.

Support doesn't come in one form, and it doesn't follow a timeline. It shifts, just as grief does.

Finding the kind of support that meets you where you are is key. For some, that means turning to family and friends—people who know your loved one, who share your memories, and who can sit with you in your pain. Their familiarity can be comforting, but it's also important to acknowledge that they may be grieving in their own way. As I've said, grief can be messy, and not everyone will be able to offer the kind of support you need. That doesn't mean they don't love you. It simply means you may need to set boundaries, communicate your needs clearly, and find additional support sources outside your inner circle.

For others, a grief support group may offer something unique. In this space, every person in the room understands loss in a way that doesn't require explanation. There is something profoundly healing about being among those who *get it*—who won't rush you to move on, who won't offer empty platitudes, but who will listen, nod, and in their silence, you know how much they understand. Whether in person or online, these communities provide validation and shared experience, offering different perspectives and coping strategies that might help lighten the weight you carry.

Professional support, such as grief counseling, provides another invaluable resource. A trained therapist can help you untangle the emotions that feel too overwhelming to face alone. They can provide tools to navigate not just grief but the guilt, regret, anger, and anxiety that often accompany it. Unlike friends or family, a therapist offers an outside perspective. You don't have to worry about being too much or saying the wrong thing in this safe space. Many religious organizations also offer grief ministries, providing compassionate community support. Whether through one-on-one counseling, group gatherings, or faith-based guidance, these ministries can comfort and understand those seeking a spiritual connection in their healing process. If your grief feels like something you can't manage on your own, seeking professional or community-based support isn't a sign of weakness, it's an act of courage.

You don't have to choose just one form of support. Healing can evolve, and your needs may shift with each step. What matters is allowing yourself to seek what serves you best in each moment. Maybe today, comfort is found in the arms of a loved one. Perhaps tomorrow, it's in the quiet understanding of a support group. Next week, it may be with the guidance of a professional who will help you navigate the depths of your sorrow. Then, years from now, it's in writing a book and sharing your story and loved one with a broad audience. There is no right or wrong way, only the path that makes you feel less alone.

ASSESSING YOUR SUPPORT NEEDS

Finding the proper support begins with understanding what feels most meaningful and helpful. Take a moment to reflect on your personal needs and preferences. Consider the following questions:

- **What type of support am I seeking?**
  - Am I seeking emotional support, practical help, or a combination?

- ○ Do I need someone to listen to me, or am I seeking guidance and advice?
- **How do I prefer to process my grief?**
  - ○ Am I comfortable sharing my emotions openly, or prefer a more private, introspective approach?
  - ○ Do I feel more supported in one-on-one conversations, small groups, or larger communities?
- **What has helped in the past, and what hasn't?**
  - ○ Have I experienced loss before? If so, what forms of support felt most healing?
  - ○ Have specific people, activities, or environments brought me comfort?
- **Who in my current circle can offer the kind of support I need?**
  - ○ Are there family members, friends, or colleagues who have been exceptionally understanding?
  - ○ Do I feel comfortable asking them for support, or must I set boundaries to protect my emotional well-being?
- **Would professional or structured support be beneficial?**
  - ○ Would speaking with a grief counselor, therapist, or religious leader provide the guidance I need?
  - ○ Would a grief support group help me feel less alone in my journey?
- **Am I open to exploring new ways of seeking support?**
  - ○ Could I benefit from creative outlets, mindfulness practices, or online support communities?
  - ○ If I've been resistant to seeking support, what's holding me back?

Not every resource or method of support will resonate with you, and that's okay. Trust your instincts—permit yourself to step back if something feels wrong. Your grief is yours to navigate, and the support you seek should align with your needs, not external expectations.

As you build your network of support, allow space for love, connection, and even moments of joy, knowing they can coexist alongside your sorrow. Each step you take in seeking support is an act of self-compassion and resilience. In honoring your healing, you also celebrate the love you shared with the one you lost. Grief does not mean you must carry their memory alone. In seeking support, you often find opportunities to share their light with others—even with strangers, allowing their love to ripple outward in ways you never expected. Each time you speak their name, tell their story, or carry forward the kindness they embodied, you extend their presence beyond loss. Healing is not about letting go; it's about finding new ways for their love to live on, both within and in the world around you.

FINDING COMMUNITY IN GRIEF

When you are forced to live without the physical presence of someone you love, the world can feel unfamiliar. The comforting rhythms of daily life are disrupted, replaced by the silence of your loved one's absence. In these moments, seeking out a community of others who have experienced similar losses can provide an unexpected balm. Engaging with those who understand the unique pain of grief can be transformative, offering a sense of belonging when everything else feels fragmented. These communities, whether formal support groups or informal gatherings of friends, create spaces where grief is acknowledged and shared. They offer a sanctuary where collective empathy and understanding lighten the burden of loss.

Consider the communities that emerged in the aftermath of the September 11, 2001 attacks in New York City. In the wake of unimaginable loss, individuals who had their lives shattered found strength in shared grief. Families, first responders, and survivors united, forging deep connections rooted in resilience, remembrance, and support. Through collective mourning and acts of solidarity, they created a network of healing that ensured the stories of their loved ones would never be forgotten and that no one had to grieve alone. These were not just gatherings of the bereaved but places where hope was nurtured, and resilience was born. The connections forged in these shared moments of sorrow became lifelines, offering support and a sense of solidarity that transcended the immediate tragedy. In these spaces, people could speak freely about their loss, knowing that their words would be met with understanding rather than pity. Sharing grief becomes a powerful form of healing, allowing individuals to express emotions that might otherwise remain unspoken.

In these communities, people share stories, shed tears, and occasionally break through the sadness with laughter. Each meeting reminds you that you are not alone in your grief and that others walk this path alongside you. Simply listening to someone else's story can provide a new perspective on your own, offering insights you might not have seen before. In these exchanges, people plant the seeds of hope, nurturing them with the collective wisdom and compassion of the group. The presence of others who truly understand your pain can be profoundly comforting, providing a sense of normalcy in a world you may no longer recognize.

The benefits of these communities extend beyond emotional support. They often become networks of practical assistance, where members help each other navigate the challenges arising from loss. Whether it's advice on dealing with legal matters, assistance with daily tasks, or simply a shoulder to cry on, these communities offer a comprehensive support system that addresses grief's emotional and practical aspects. The bonds formed here can last a lifetime, providing ongoing support long after the initial shock of loss has passed.

For some, the idea of joining a community is daunting. The thought of sharing your innermost feelings with strangers can be intimidating. Yet, it's important to remember that these spaces are filled with people who understand your hesitation, having likely felt the same way. The strength of these communities lies in their diversity, with each member bringing their own experiences and insights to the table. This diversity enriches the group, offering a wider range of perspectives and coping strategies that can be invaluable in navigating grief.

If you're considering joining a community, take the time to explore different options. Some people find comfort in groups that focus on specific types of loss. In contrast, others prefer more general grief support settings. There are also online communities offering support from the comfort of your home, providing a sense of connection even in isolation. Whatever form it takes, the right community can become integral to your healing process, offering companionship and understanding as you move forward.

In the end, finding a community that resonates with you can be crucial in the healing process. It provides a space where you can be yourself, free from the outside world's expectations. Here, you can share your grief without fear of judgment, knowing you are surrounded by others who understand. These communities offer a powerful reminder that while grief is a deeply personal experience, it can be shared, transforming isolation into connection and despair into hope.

NAVIGATING SUPPORT GROUPS

Choosing the right support group is a delicate process, requiring a thoughtful approach to finding a space that genuinely resonates with your needs. Each group has its unique composition, and aligning yourself with individuals who have experienced similar types of loss is essential. This shared understanding fosters empathy and connection, making you feel seen and heard in ways difficult to articulate to those who haven't experienced similar loss. When you enter a room filled with others who understand the brand of grief you carry, an unspoken bond forms. This bond can be incredibly healing, offering a haven where vulnerability meets with compassion and shared experiences become a source of strength.

Facilitation style is another crucial aspect to consider when selecting a support group. Some groups are led by professional therapists who bring expertise and structure to the sessions, guiding conversations and ensuring the environment remains supportive and constructive. These therapists can provide valuable insights and coping strategies, helping you work through the complex emotions that accompany grief. On the other hand, peer-facilitated groups offer a different dynamic that emphasizes mutual support and shared leadership. In these settings, the participants drive the conversation, drawing on their collective wisdom to navigate the challenges of loss. The choice between these styles depends on your comfort level and what you hope to gain from the experience. A therapist-led group may be ideal if you prefer a more structured approach. However, if you're looking for a space to share and learn from others in a more organic way, a peer-facilitated group might be the right fit.

Group dynamics play a significant role in shaping your experience within a support group. Attending a session or two is important to observe how the group interacts and whether the atmosphere aligns with your preferences for sharing and receiving support. Pay attention to how the facilitator guides the discussion and how participants respond to one another. Are conversations respectful and inclusive? Do you feel comfortable sharing your story and emotions? The group dynamics can significantly influence your sense of belonging and the effectiveness of the support you receive. Trust your instincts; if something doesn't feel right, exploring other options is okay until you find a group where you feel genuinely at ease.

While the support group environment can be incredibly nurturing, it's important to recognize that not every group will be the right fit. Try a few different groups before finding one that truly resonates with you. This exploration is a normal part of the process, and it's okay to move on if a group doesn't meet your needs. Your comfort and sense of safety are paramount, and finding a group that respects your boundaries and supports your healing journey is essential. As you navigate the world of support groups, remain open to the possibilities they offer. The right group can become a cornerstone of your healing process, providing the companionship and understanding that make the weight of grief a little more bearable.

A LIFE SUSPENDED: THE WEIGHT OF COMPLICATED GRIEF

The dishes sat in the sink, untouched for weeks. The mail was piled up by the front door, unopened and collecting dust. In the dim quiet of the house, Logan sat in the same chair he had occupied every night for months, staring at the same framed picture of his wife, Elise. The edges of the frame were smudged from where his fingers had traced it over and over, a ritual that both comforted and tormented him. It had been almost a year since the accident, but time had not moved forward for him. The world outside kept spinning—people went to work, laughed at coffee shops, celebrated birthdays—but inside, Logan remained frozen in the moment his life shattered.

Grief is a natural response to losing someone we love, a testament to the depth of our connection. Yet, there are times when the weight of this grief becomes too heavy to carry alone. What Logan was experiencing wasn't just grief; it was something deeper, something that wrapped around him so tightly he could no longer breathe. His loss had become his identity. He no longer saw himself as a husband, a friend, or a colleague—he was simply a man whose wife had died. And in some ways, he felt like he had died with her.

At first, people had tried to reach out. His sister, Camille, had called every day, gently urging him to come over for dinner, to get out of the house. His best friend, Nate, had invited him to their usual Sunday morning coffee runs, the same ones he and Elise used to go on together. But Logan ignored the calls and let the messages go unanswered. He convinced himself that no one could understand, that engaging with the world meant betraying his pain. He stopped showing up to work, making excuses until the emails from his boss eventually stopped coming. Social withdrawal is a typical response to grief. Still, when it extends beyond the initial grieving period, it may indicate the need for counseling. Yet, the idea of help felt impossible, like no therapist could say anything that would make this feel any less unbearable.

Logan wasn't just mourning Elise; he was caught in a loop of *if only* and *what ifs*. Intrusive thoughts invaded his mind relentlessly, disrupting his ability to function. If only he had driven her to work that morning instead of letting her take the bus. What if he had convinced her to call in sick, stay home, and do anything except be in the wrong place at the wrong time? The replay never stopped, as if punishing himself could bring her back. These thoughts weren't just passing grief, they consumed him, keeping him trapped in a cycle of regret.

One night, after another evening of staring at the picture, Logan poured himself a glass of whiskey. Then another. And another. The alcohol dulled the sharp edges of his pain, offering a temporary escape from the grief that clung to him like a second skin. Substance abuse is a serious sign that professional help is needed. What started as an occasional drink to numb the loneliness became an anchor, dragging him deeper into his despair. Grief had not just taken Elise; it was taking Logan, too.

BREAKING THE CYCLE: SEEKING SUPPORT

One afternoon, his sister, Camille, showed up unannounced. She didn't tell him to move on. She didn't tell him that Elise would want him to be happy. She just sat with him in silence. And then, after a long pause, she said, *"Logan, I love you. But I can't sit back and watch you disappear. Elise wouldn't want this for you. And I know you don't want this for yourself either."*

He wanted to argue, to tell her she didn't understand—but deep down, something in her words hit him like a gust of air in a drowning moment. It was the first time he let himself imagine something beyond his pain.

Camille helped him find a grief counselor, someone who wouldn't force him to "move on" but who would sit with him in the weight of his sorrow and help him navigate through it. Grief emotions can fluctuate wildly, and if overwhelming emotions refuse to subside, professional support can provide a framework for healing. At first, therapy felt pointless. He sat in the office, arms crossed, silent. But slowly, session by session, he started to speak.

He learned that his mind, in an attempt to make sense of Elise's death, was trying to blame someone where there was no one to blame. His therapist helped him recognize that *complicated grief* wasn't just about missing Elise—it was about feeling responsible for something he could never have controlled. That realization didn't erase the pain, but it loosened its grip ever so slightly.

A PATH FORWARD

Therapy didn't magically make Logan's grief disappear. But it gave him the tools to begin living again. His therapist encouraged him to take small steps, answer one text message, step outside for five minutes, and reintroduce himself to something that once brought him joy. Healing wasn't about forgetting Elise but learning to carry her memory without letting it consume him.

One morning, Logan found himself at the café he and Elise used to visit. The seat across from him was empty, but for the first time in months, he didn't turn away from it. He took a deep breath, let the grief sit beside him—but he also let in the warmth of the sun streaming through the window, the aroma of fresh coffee, the quiet hum of life moving forward.

Grief, especially when complicated, can feel endless. But support, whether from family, friends, or professional counseling, can offer a way through. Seeking help isn't about erasing the pain; it's about finding a way to live alongside it without letting it take everything. Perhaps most importantly, it's about allowing love to be the wind beneath your wings.

As we move forward, we will explore how seeking support isn't just about survival—it's about finding ways to reconnect with meaning and purpose, even in the face of profound loss.

9
THE JOURNEY OF
TRANSFORMATION

In the stillness of my life, I often find myself reflecting on the way grief has reshaped me. At first, it felt like a weight that could never be lifted, an endless night with no promise of dawn. But over time, amid the heartbreak and devastation, an unexpected light began to flicker—dim at first but undeniably present. It was a light born not from forgetting or moving on but from the deep love that loss could never erase.

I've realized that while the length of time we have with loved ones is not ours to choose, their presence is an extraordinary gift. No matter how brief or enduring, every relationship carries a profound impact —one that imprints on our hearts, shaping who we are and how we love. The moments we shared, the lessons they taught us, the laughter, the struggles, the quiet, everyday tenderness, these are not lost with time. They remain woven into the fabric of our lives, guiding us in ways we may not fully understand.

The duration of a relationship does not determine its significance. A lifetime of love can be experienced in just a few years; a single moment can hold more meaning than decades. And though grief aches for more time, the true gift is that we had them at all. Their love, their presence, the way they changed us, these are the things that endure. And as we carry them forward, their love shapes the world through us.

And grief, I've learned, is not merely an endpoint. It is a force of transformation, an invitation to step into a space of vulnerability and courage. It asks us to confront our pain, to let it shape us, to learn from it, and to find meaning in a world forever changed. In many ways, grief has been my greatest teacher. It has shattered me but expanded me, showing me depths of resilience, love, and understanding I never knew I possessed.

TWO LOSSES THAT SHAPED ME

There have been two defining moments in my life when grief came and changed everything. First, the loss of my father came with the painful gift of time. The second, the loss of my daughter, came without warning, without mercy, without a chance to say goodbye.

LOSING MY FATHER: THE SLOW GOODBYE

When my dad was diagnosed with pancreatic cancer, I knew our time together was running out. And because I knew, I could say everything I wanted him to know. I told him how much I loved him, how much I appreciated him, and how grateful I was for everything he had given me: the wisdom, the strength, the unwavering support.

"Bend like the willow tree," he told me. *"Life will throw storms your way, but don't let them break you."*

I held onto those words when he passed. I told myself I was prepared. But when the moment came, I realized that no preparation could soften the loss. I missed him on holidays, at family gatherings, and in the quiet, ordinary moments when I wanted to hear his voice.

I missed watching him love my children and seeing him be the grandfather I knew he would have been. I missed the way he made me feel steady and safe at home.

But in the wake of his passing, I carried his lessons with me. He taught me resilience, which allowed me to bend but not break. And that lesson would become all the more critical when grief struck again in a way I never could have prepared for.

LOSING MY DAUGHTER: THE UNTHINKABLE LOSS

Losing my father was painful, but I understood it. I could make sense of it. Losing Jenna was something else entirely. One moment, she was here, full of life, laughter, and endless possibilities. The next, she was gone, just gone.

There was no time to prepare, no slow goodbye. I had no moment to hold her hand and tell her everything I wanted her to know. I didn't get to thank her for making me a mother; it was an honor. I didn't get to say I'm so sorry for not always getting the parenting thing right. The ache of losing her is something I never knew a person could survive. I didn't just grieve her absence; I grieved the future she never got to have. The milestones she would never reach. The life she was supposed to live. I grieved for myself. I grieved for my husband. I grieved for my younger daughters. I grieved for our family, and I grieved for her friends. Not only that, but I grieved for all the moments of hers we would never get to share, for the mother I was supposed to be for her until the day I died.

Her loss shook me to my core. It changed everything. But amid the devastation, I found that grief had something to teach me again.

Jenna made me a better person. In losing her, I gained a depth of compassion I never knew I had. I became more giving, more present, more intentional with my love. At the same time, I lost patience for the superficial—the petty dramas, the meaningless noise. My priorities shifted. I grew in ways that I never expected, both spiritually and mentally.

Grief shaped me, but it did not define me. And more importantly, it did not define Jenna's legacy. Because her light—her love—is still here. It lives in me and our family.

GRIEF AS A CATALYST FOR GROWTH

Grief strips everything away. It takes you to your rawest form, forcing you to see what remains. And in that space, you have a choice. You can let it consume you, or you can let it transform you.

For me, grief led to deep reflection. It made me question what truly mattered. It forced me to reevaluate my values, my purpose, my way of being in the world.

Through loss, I have learned:

- **Resilience** is not about never falling but rising again, even when you don't know how.
- **Love** is not bound by time or physical presence; it continues endlessly in how we carry those who have passed before us.
- **Perspective** changes—grief teaches us to hold onto what truly matters and let go of what does not.
- **Growth** is possible, even in the darkest of times.

Each of us walks a unique grief journey, but we do not walk it alone. As we move through loss, we find new ways to live, love, and honor those who are no longer physically with us.

THE POWER OF CHOICE IN GRIEF

Grief will shape you, but how it shapes you is your choice. You can choose to remain in the pain, or you can choose to coexist with it, allowing the love that still exists to guide you forward. You can choose to be bitter, or you can choose to be open.

Grief will shape you—there is no escaping that truth—but you have the power to decide *how* it defines you. You can let it anchor you in sorrow, or you can allow the love you will forever share to be the force that carries you into the future with light, gratitude, and joy leading the way.

Jenna and my dad are still with me. Not in the way I wish they were, but still in a way that very much matters:

- They are in the way I love my family.
- They are in the way I choose kindness over anger.
- They are in the way I show up for others who are grieving because I know what it means to hurt this deeply.
- They are in the way I live.
- They are how I cherish the small, fleeting moments— because I now understand tomorrow is never promised.
- They are in the way I speak their names, keeping their stories alive in the hearts of others.
- They are how I choose love over fear, embracing life even in uncertainty.
- They are in the way I forgive, knowing that holding onto resentment only weighs me down.
- They are in the way I find beauty in the ordinary, in sunsets, laughter, and the quiet presence of those I love.
- They are in the way I give, not just because I can, but because generosity is one of the greatest ways to honor them.
- They are in the way I choose to live fully—to go on adventures, make memories, and say yes to the experiences they never got to have.
- They are in how I keep searching for meaning, growth, and

a way to transform loss into something that can light the path for others.

And that is their legacy.

AN INVITATION TO YOU

If you are reading this, then you, too, have walked through grief. You, too, have felt the weight of loss. And I hope that in these pages, you have found something that resonates with you—a reminder that you are not alone, that your grief is valid, that your love endures.

You do not have to be the same person you were before your loss. You are allowed to change, to grow, to let grief reshape you into someone who loves even more deeply. And most of all, you are allowed to live. Because in living, you carry them with you. And in that, they are never truly gone.

REBIRTH AND REDISCOVERY

Loss changes us. It alters the landscape of our lives in ways we never expected, forcing us to navigate a world that no longer looks or feels the same. At first, moving forward can feel like a betrayal—like letting go of the person we love. But in time, we can understand that moving forward is not about leaving them behind; it's about carrying them with us in new and meaningful ways.

Grief strips away the illusion of permanence, revealing what truly matters. It shakes the foundation of our beliefs, routines, and priorities and asks us to look deeper. What once seemed important may now feel insignificant, while things we previously overlooked begin to call to us. This is the space where transformation begins—not in forgetting, but in rediscovering who we are in the wake of loss.

As you step into this uncharted territory, you may find yourself drawn to new interests that resonate with your evolving self. Perhaps there is a passion you set aside, a curiosity you never explored, or a skill you've always wanted to learn. These pursuits are not distractions from grief but expressions of growth—ways to honor life in all its complexity. Whether painting, hiking, writing, or learning to play an instrument, embracing new experiences can be healing and empowering, a reminder that life still holds moments of beauty and purpose.

Just as grief reshapes our internal world, it also reshapes our relationships. Some connections deepen as shared vulnerability fosters understanding and support. Others may naturally fade if they no longer align with the person you are becoming. This is a time to surround yourself with people who nurture your spirit, those who can sit with your sorrow and joy without rushing you to be anything other than what you are now.

For many, grief prompts a reevaluation of life's direction. Losing a loved one may stir questions about career paths, living arrangements, or even deeper existential purposes. You may feel called to shift gears, seek more meaningful work, relocate, engage in volunteerism, or build something new in their honor. These changes are not about abandoning the past but integrating it into a life that reflects the love and wisdom your shared love has imparted to you.

Most importantly, this rebirth phase is not about forcing yourself to "move on"—because you don't have to. Instead, it's about moving with your grief, allowing it to be part of you while shaping your evolution. Grief will change you—that is inevitable—but you can guide that transformation toward something meaningful through awareness and intention. Your loved one's presence is not lost; it is woven into your choices, the love you give, and the courage you show in embracing life again. They are not left behind; they are carried forward in how you live, allowing their love to guide every step forward.

This journey is not linear. There will be moments when grief resurfaces when the weight of loss feels as heavy as it did in the beginning. But with time, those moments become interwoven with something else—gratitude, resilience, even joy. The pain does not disappear, but it no longer overshadows everything. Instead, it becomes part of a larger tapestry that includes love and loss, sorrow and beauty, endings and beginnings.

Rediscovery is about allowing yourself to hold both grief and possibility simultaneously. It is about making space for new experiences, laughter, and moments of light that coexist with sadness. It is about stepping forward with intention, not because you are leaving your loved one behind, but because their love continues to shape the path ahead.

And as you take those steps—tentative at first, then with growing confidence—you may come to see that rebirth is not about becoming someone new. It's about becoming more fully yourself, shaped by the love you shared and the lessons your loss taught you. Your story is still unfolding. And your loved one will forever be a part of it.

FINDING LIGHT IN THE DARKNESS

In the depths of grief, it can feel as though light no longer exists—as if the sun has set and forgotten to rise again, leaving you in an endless night. The warmth and radiance that once filled your world may feel like they have vanished, replaced by a heavy stillness. But just as the sun is never truly gone, only hidden behind the horizon, light still exists in your life—it is simply waiting to return, in its own time, in ways you may not yet see.

This is not about replacing pain with happiness or forcing yourself to move on. It is about gently letting the light back, making space for both sorrow and joy, for longing and gratitude, for the past that shaped you and the future still waiting to unfold. Just as a room darkened by grief can slowly brighten when you open the windows, your heart, too, can welcome light without erasing the love that loss has etched into your soul.

Reconnecting with small moments of light can be as simple as:

- **Engaging in activities that bring you peace.** A walk outside, a quiet morning with a book, or revisiting an old hobby can help anchor you in the present.
- **Reaching out to others.** Grief can feel isolating, but relationships can be a source of comfort. Whether through family, friends, or community, human connection reminds us we are not alone.
- **Practicing gratitude.** Even amid loss, there are moments of goodness—small but significant. A warm embrace, hot water in the shower, a cherished memory, or the kindness of a stranger. Acknowledging these moments does not erase pain but creates a healing space.
- **Allowing joy without guilt.** The moments of happiness you experience do not diminish the depth of your loss. They honor the love you carry by proving that it endures.

Finding light in the darkness does not mean that grief disappears. It means learning to walk with it in a way that allows love to guide you. It is about stepping into life not despite your loss but because the love you share is still with you, urging you to live in a way that honors all that was, and all that still is.

As you move forward, trust your ability to hold life's sorrow and beauty. Your love will always be a guiding force, a light that cannot be extinguished, even on the darkest nights.

KEEPING THE CONVERSATION ALIVE

Now that you've walked through these pages—through the messy, complicated, and deeply human experience of grief, I hope you feel a little less alone. I hope you've found space for your loss, for your love, and for the voice inside you that deserves to be heard.

But this journey isn't just yours.

There's someone out there searching for the right words, for a sign that they're not the only one who feels this way. **Your review could be the nudge they need to pick up this book and find the support they're looking for.**

By sharing your honest thoughts on Amazon, you're not just helping me—you're helping someone else who needs to know they're not alone in this.

To leave a review, simply scan the QR code or visit:

SCAN ME

Thank you for keeping this conversation alive. **Grief, love, and healing are meant to be shared.**

With gratitude,

Dena M. Derenale Betti

CONCLUSION

As we reach the final pages of this book, thank you for walking this journey with me. Grief is deeply personal, yet it connects us in unexpected ways. If there's one thing I hope you take from these pages, grief is not just an end but a transformation. It changes you, but you have a say in how it shapes you.

Sometimes, we have time to prepare—we see it coming, and while it doesn't soften the pain, it allows us space to say goodbye, express our love, and hold on to the final moments. Other times, the loss is sudden, shattering our world in an instant, leaving us grappling with unanswered questions and an ache we never imagined we could endure. No two experiences of loss are the same, yet they all change us.

This book was written to meet you wherever you are in your grief and offers understanding, tools, and encouragement as you navigate your path. It is not a roadmap to "moving on" but an invitation to move forward with love as your guiding light. Through these pages, I hope you've discovered ways to acknowledge your pain while also making space for healing, to honor your loved one not just in sorrow but in the way you continue to live.

Grief, at its core, is a reflection of love. And while we don't get to choose how long someone remains in our lives, we can choose how we carry their memory. Please take from this journey the ability to see the gift of each person who has touched your life. May you allow their love to shape you, strengthen you, and remind you that even in the face of loss, your story—and theirs—continues.

You, too, have this choice. Grief may reshape you, but it does not have to diminish you. When grief and loss won't shut up—when they echo through your mind, refusing to fade, I hope these pages have provided you a compass to navigate the storm within. A way to hold space for sorrow and love at the same time. A way to acknowledge your pain while also making room for joy. You can honor the one you lost not by staying in the darkness but by allowing their love to be the light that guides you forward.

And if you are seeking support as you navigate this path, please know you do not have to do it alone. My family and I created *#hersmile Nonprofit* in Jenna's honor, a community built on love, resilience, and connection. I invite you to visit **hersmile.org** to find support, resources, and ways to honor your loved one's memory. Whether you need a place to share your story, a community to walk alongside you, or simply reassurance that healing is possible, we are here.

Thank you for trusting me with your heart, allowing me to share my story and the stories of those who have crossed my path, and embracing your path with courage. Your journey is still unfolding, and I hope you continue to choose love, seek light, and honor the beauty of the life you are meant to live.

With love and gratitude,

Dena M. Derenale Betti

NOTES

- Lewis, C.S. *A Grief Observed*. Harper One, 2009.
- Didion, Joan. *The Year of Magical Thinking*. Alfred A. Knopf, 2005.
- van der Kolk, Bessel. *The Body Keeps the Score: Brain, Mind, and Body in the Healing of Trauma*. Viking, 2014.
- Devine, Megan. *It's OK That You're Not OK: Meeting Grief and Loss in a Culture That Doesn't Understand*. Sounds True, 2017.
- McRaven, William H. *Make Your Bed: Little Things That Can Change Your Life...And Maybe the World*. Grand Central Publishing, 2017.
- Tolle, Eckhart. *The Power of Now: A Guide to Spiritual Enlightenment*. Namaste Publishing, 1999.
- Kubany, E. S., & Manke, F. P. (1995). Cognitive distortions and guilt in the context of traumatic grief: A preliminary examination. *Anxiety, Stress & Coping, 8*(4), 309-322. Neimeyer, R. A. (2001). *The language of loss: A guide to understanding the work of mourning*. Westview Press.
- Clegg, Bill. *Did You Ever Have a Family*. Gallery/Scout Press, 2015.
- Enright, R. (2024, November 1). *From Grief to Acceptance: How to Find Healing After Loss*. Psychology Today. https://www.psychologytoday.com/us/blog/focus-on-forgiveness/202411/from-grief-to-acceptance-how-to-find-healing-after-loss
- SuperSummary Editorial Team. (n.d.). *A Grief Observed Summary and Study Guide*. SuperSummary. https://www.supersummary.com/a-grief-observed/summary/
- Growth Through Grief Organization. (n.d.). *The Body Keeps Score: The Impact of Grief on Your Health*. Growth Through Grief. https://growththroughgrief.org/the-body-keeps-score-the-impact-of-grief-on-your-health/
- SparkNotes Editors. (n.d.). *The Year of Magical Thinking: Themes*. SparkNotes. https://www.sparknotes.com/lit/yearmagical/themes/
- Blanchard, M.K., & Runkle, M.J. (2023, July 4). *Kubler-Ross Stages of Dying and Subsequent Models*. National Center for Biotechnology Information. https://www.ncbi.nlm.nih.gov/books/NBK507885/
- Harvard Health Publishing. (2023, March 1). *5 Stages of Grief: Coping with the Loss of a Loved One*. Harvard Health. https://www.health.harvard.edu/mind-and-mood/5-stages-of-grief-coping-with-the-loss-of-a-loved-one

- National Institute on Aging. (2023, April 14). Coping With Grief and Loss. National Institute on Aging. *https://www.nia.nih.gov/health/grief-and-mourning/coping-grief-and-loss*
- O'Connor, M., & Wagner, B. (2021, May 27). *What is Good Grief Support? Exploring the Actors and Actions in Social Support After Traumatic Grief.* National Institutes of Health. https://www.ncbi.nlm.nih.gov/pmc/articles/PMC8158955/
- Centers for Disease Control and Prevention. (2021, April 29). *Health Effects of Social Isolation and Loneliness.* CDC. https://www.cdc.gov/social-connectedness/risk-factors/index.html
- Wolfelt, A. (2015, October). *Introduction: A Declaration of My Intent. Center for Loss.* https://www.centerforloss.com/wp-content/uploads/2015/10/Introduction-to-Companioning-the-Bereaved-by-Dr-Alan-Wolfelt.pdf
- Grief Stories Team. (n.d.). *Creative Outlets for Grief.* Grief Stories. https://www.griefstories.org/creative-outlets-for-grief/
- Illume Apps. (n.d.). *Grief in Different Cultures and Religions.* Illume Apps. https://illumeapps.com/griefworks-blog/grief-in-different-cultures-and-religions/
- Haley, E., & Williams, L. (2018, August 20). *Setting Boundaries While Grieving. What's Your Grief?* https://whatsyourgrief.com/setting-boundaries-grief-boundaries/
- American Psychological Association. (n.d.). *Apprehending the Concept of Resilience.* APA. https://www.apa.org/ed/precollege/topss/daily-life-resilience.pdf
- Healthline Editorial Team. (2020, April 30). *Present Tense: 7 Mindfulness Strategies to Cope with Loss.* Healthline. https://www.healthline.com/health/mind-body/mindfulness-strategies-to-cope-with-loss
- Devine, M. (2021, January 5). *How Journaling Can Help You Grieve.* Psychology Today. https://www.psychologytoday.com/us/blog/understanding-grief/202101/how-journaling-can-help-you-grieve
- Therapist Aid. (n.d.). *Grief Rituals | Article.* Therapist Aid. https://www.therapistaid.com/therapy-article/grief-rituals
- Eterneva Team. (n.d.). *6 Legacy Project Ideas to Honor Your Loved Ones.* Eterneva. https://www.eterneva.com/resources/legacy-project-ideas
- Stroebe, M., & Schut, H. (2001). *The Dual Process Model of Coping with Bereavement.* PubMed. https://pubmed.ncbi.nlm.nih.gov/10848151/
- On The Way To Where You're Going Team. (n.d.). *50 Creative Ways to Honor a Deceased Loved One.* On The Way To Where You're Going. https://onthewaytowhereyouregoing.com/honor-your-loved-one/

- Holocaust Memorial Day Trust. (n.d.). *Lily Ebert MBE*. HMD. https://hmd. org.uk/resource/lily-ebert/
- The West Australian. (2021, March 13). *How Marite Norris Brought Colour Back into Her World After Losing Children Mo, Evie, and Otis in MH17*. The West Australian. https://thewest.com.au/lifestyle/stm/how-marite-norris-brought-colour-back-into-her-world-after-losing-children-mo-evie-and-otis-in-mh17-c-14525184
- Schlossberg, N.K. (2024, December 12). *Finding Joy Amid Grief While Navigating the Holidays*. Psychology Today. https://www.psychologytoday. com/us/blog/aging-with-purpose/202412/finding-joy-amid-grief-while-navigating-the-holidays
- Marques, L. (2022, October 6). *How Can You Find Joy (or at Least Peace) During Difficult Times?* Harvard Health. https://www.health.harvard.edu/ blog/how-can-you-find-joy-or-at-least-peace-during-difficult-times-202210062826
- Meekhof, K. (2023, May 15). *Learn to Let Go of Guilt in Grief*. Psychology Today. https://www.psychologytoday.com/us/blog/widows-walk/202305/ learn-to-let-go-of-guilt-in-grief
- Haley, E., & Williams, L. (2019, April 10). *The Important Distinction Between Guilt and Regret in Grief*. Whats Your Grief. https://whatsyourgrief.com/ guilt-vs-regret-in-grief/
- Ackerman, C.E. (2020, July 10). *Fostering Self-Forgiveness: 25 Powerful Techniques and Books*. Positive Psychology. https://positivepsychology.com/ self-forgiveness/
- Crane, M. (2018, November 6). *Mindfulness Apps: How Well Do They Work?* Harvard Health. https://www.health.harvard.edu/blog/mindfulness-apps-how-well-do-they-work-2018110615306
- Dyregrov, K., & Dyregrov, A. (2020, August 20). *Experiences of Participation in Bereavement Groups from Significant Others' Perspectives: A Qualitative Study*. National Institutes of Health. https://www.ncbi.nlm.nih.gov/pmc/ articles/PMC7429679/
- Grant, H. (2024, September 2). *The Grenfell Communities Sharing Solace and Succour*. The Guardian. https://www.theguardian.com/uk-news/article/ 2024/sep/02/gathered-in-grief-the-grenfell-communities-sharing-solace-and-succour
- Mayo Clinic Staff. (2018, June 19). *Complicated Grief - Symptoms and Causes*. Mayo Clinic. https://www.mayoclinic.org/diseases-conditions/ complicated-grief/symptoms-causes/syc-20360374
- Sutton, J. (2021, April 9). *10 Grief Counseling Therapy Techniques &*

Interventions. Positive Psychology. https://positivepsychology.com/grief-counseling/

- Various Researchers. (2023, March 24). *Posttraumatic Growth After Perinatal Loss: A Systematic Review.* PubMed. https://pubmed.ncbi.nlm.nih.

ABOUT THE AUTHOR

Dena M. Derenale Betti is a mother, a wife, a friend, and someone who knows the weight of love and loss. Life has given her both incredible joy and unimaginable heartbreak, shaping the way she sees the world and the way she chooses to move through it.

She never imagined she'd be writing about grief. But when her 14-year-old daughter, Jenna, passed away, everything changed. Grief cracked her wide open, forcing her to reimagine what it means to survive, to love, and to keep going when the world as she knew it was gone. That loss became the catalyst for #hersmile, a nonprofit dedicated to helping families who have lost a child or a parent with dependent children. Through #hersmile, Dena has found a way to turn heartbreak into something bigger—something that offers hope, connection, and a way forward for those lost in loss.

Dena's background isn't in counseling or therapy. She started her career as a real estate appraiser and later stepped into the world of digital marketing. But none of that prepared her for the lessons grief would teach her. Now, she uses her skills to amplify the voices of those who need to be heard, to spread messages of resilience, and to remind people that they are not alone.

She studied at the University of San Francisco, where she played on the school's first women's golf team and earned a Bachelor of Science degree. But the lessons that shaped her the most didn't come from textbooks—they came from love, loss, and the unwavering belief that even in the darkest moments, light still finds a way in.

Dena is also the author of *You Are Stronger Than You Know: My Daughter Told Me So*, a book born from the wisdom of grief and the love that never fades.

Because in the end, that's what she believes most: **love never leaves. It simply changes form.**

Printed in Dunstable, United Kingdom

64292614R00109